In Bloom

Kayla Aimee

In Bloom

Trading Restless Insecurity
for Abiding Confidence

B&H
PUBLISHING GROUP

NASHVILLE, TENNESSEE

Published by B&H Publishing Group
Nashville, Tennessee

Published in association with literary agent Jenni Burke
of D.C. Jacobson & Associations, LLC, an Author
Management Company, www.dcjacobson.com.

Dewey Decimal Classification: 248.843
Subject Heading: WOMEN / SELF-CONFIDENCE /
SELF-PERCEPTION

Cover design by Jennifer Allison, Studio Nth.

1 2 3 4 5 6 7 • 22 21 20 19 18

To Ridley
For showing me the transformative magic of a new season

And to Scarlette
For teaching me how to flourish

Contents

Introduction   1

Chapter 1. Uninvited   7
Chapter 2. Rejected   13
Chapter 3. Consumed   23
Chapter 4. Squad Goals   31
Chapter 5. Making Out   41
Chapter 6. Between the Sheets   49
Chapter 7. Piece of Glass   61
Chapter 8. Abandoned   71
Chapter 9. I Love the Nineties   81
Chapter 10. Inside Out   89
Chapter 11. Thief of Joy   99
Chapter 12. Measuring Up   109
Chapter 13. For Such a Time as This   119
Chapter 14. What Are You Afraid Of?   127
Chapter 15. Metamorphosis   137
Chapter 16. Great Expectations   145
Chapter 17. Rewriting the Girl Code   151
Chapter 18. Judgment Day   161
Chapter 19. Harvest   171
Chapter 20. Flourish   177

Acknowledgments   185
Study Guide for Individuals and Small Groups   187
Notes   193

Introduction

Therefore, if anyone is in Christ, he is a new creation; the
old has passed away, and see, the new has come!
—2 Corinthians 5:17

My shoes were all wrong. Black Mary Janes with wide straps, they betrayed me with their sparkly sequins, catching the light from the classroom windows and reflecting it back on row upon row of matching white tennis shoes with three-and-a-half-inch rubber heels. I slid down further in my seat, tucking my toes under my backpack as a faint blush crept over my cheeks. Maybe no one would notice.

I glanced around furtively to assess the footwear situation of the rest of my classmates. White, chunky-heeled platform tennis shoes, white tennis shoes, white tennis shoes. What was this, gym class? Did everyone assume we'd be doing first serves instead of first period today?

As I surveyed the sea of white platform heels, the most popular girl in our grade caught my eye, glancing down at the floor where I was self-consciously attempting to wedge my feet further under my backpack to hide my obviously uncool footwear choices. She smirked and bent her head close to the girl next to her, her chestnut brown hair swaying as she tilted her head in my direction. Thick and glossy, with artfully arranged little butterfly clips across the crown as though it was meant to look casual but must have taken all morning to pin in place, her hair fell across her face, blocking her from view but not quite muffling the sounds of the two of them giggling.

How did everyone even know what shoes to buy anyway? I mean, was there some sort of seventh-grade girl newsletter that circulated during the summer? "To be considered cool, buy these shoes"?

I had been trying hard to prepare for junior high. First, I convinced my mom to let me buy all those teen magazines (okay, so I hid some in the cart and snuck them on the conveyor belt when she wasn't looking), and then I mapped out elaborate charts with the coolest outfits I could afford on my meager babysitting salary. Like a vision board. I saw that on *Oprah*. I took a copy of *Seventeen* with me when I was shopping for a back-to-school wardrobe that *should* have made the cute boy in homeroom notice me. I blew basically my entire budget on those sequined Mary Janes in Delia's, as seen on page forty-three. They were supposed to be THE thing that year. And okay, they totally did make my legs look longer.

But apparently, they were not the "Must Have Item for School" like the September issue promised because, hello! White tennis shoes with three-inch heels. Where was THAT piece of information, *Seventeen* magazine? Those magazines were full of lies. No one even tried to kiss me by my locker either. I'm probably going to sue.

The bell rang, and as I gathered up all my books to leave, I felt a hard shove from behind, then blushed again as I bent to pick up the scattered contents of my Sanrio pencil box from the floor. Popular Girl smirked down at me as she passed. "Loser," she hissed, and then tossed her head and laughed as she flounced off in her white, chunky-heeled tennis shoes.

Loser.

I reached out and caught that word as it hung in the air between us. I absorbed its weight, and it quickly made a home in me. I didn't know who I was yet, but I knew that this word had correctly defined me. This one moment reflected back all the insecurities I already had about myself, which meant it must be true. And so I believed it easily, without question.

———❦

Maybe you are like me. Maybe someone else's words have reduced you. Maybe you've been made to feel invisible or inferior or inadequate or ashamed. Shame is like Stockholm syndrome. It holds us hostage, and after a while we subconsciously embrace it because it's become our method of survival. Shame is our captor, and we were never meant to be held captive. We were meant to be captivated. God promises to restore the years the locusts have eaten, avows in Isaiah that "in place of your shame, you will have a double portion" (61:7). Our entire covenant is based on redemption. And the Bible holds the blueprint to interrupt our insecurity.

———

I spent my formative years in a cycle of feeling hopelessly uncool.

All I ever wanted was to be a cool girl, to shed the wrapping of shame and live with confidence. I checked out books from the library on the topic, even underlining and highlighting one titled *How to Be Popular*. I totally tried flirtatiously dropping my pencil in front of the cute boy who sat behind me, but surprisingly he didn't ask me to be his date to homecoming, thereby cementing my place among the cool kids. Instead, he just wordlessly handed the pencil back to me and simultaneously shattered all of my dreams (as well as my trust in coming-of-age films). No makeover. No debut of my ugly-duckling-to-swan transformation in front of his friends. Nothing.

From the moment the glossy-haired girl discarded me with her once-over, I embraced a new sense of self-worth that felt less-than, cast aside, and rejected. It felt shameful just to *be* me, even if I didn't understand why. And the thing about shame is that it seeps so deeply, rooting so firmly within us, that it becomes enmeshed with who we are. It becomes a filter we don't even realize we've layered over the top of our feelings and responses. It becomes our reason *for* rather than our reason *why not*.

And once it takes root, it breeds an insecurity that colors all of our interactions.

As an adult I listened to Brené Brown on stage at a TED talk, describing shame as "the intensely painful feeling or experience of believing that we are flawed and therefore unworthy of love and belonging."[1] I heard it as the definition of how I was living. Shame in action strips us of our confidence. It decimates our self-worth. Worst of all, it distorts the truth of who we were created to be. It ensnares us with its subtle lies, leaving us longing and lonely. Somewhere along the way I collected all the tiny moments of hurt and embarrassment and insecurity, and I decided they comprised who I was. I was like a sieve. All the good things and encouraging words passed through me like water, leaving only the muck behind.

I felt worse than invisible: I felt insignificant. And like many women I know, I buried the beauty that was uniquely knit into me by my Creator when He formed me "in my mother's womb" (Ps. 139:13). I quit nourishing the gifts that were waiting to bloom within me. I believed in a good God but missed connecting His goodness to who I was.

Shame keeps us striving for acceptance, but grace gives us eternal belonging. This is where everything turns around. This is how we unlock the mystery. This is where we rewrite the girl code and change our heart narrative to mimic the Almighty instead of the mean girls. The good news is in the Good News. You can only get two chapters into the Word before it comes spilling out, "Both the man and his wife were naked, yet felt no shame" (Gen. 2:25). This is how life began, in our Eden, naked and unashamed. This is more than a longing; this is how we were created to be. This is the divine design of our humanity, that we would live with one another uncovered and unburdened.

For years I stayed locked inside myself, and then I swelled full and gave birth to new life. As I held my newborn daughter in my arms, I knew I had to conquer my battle with insecurity for *her* sake, so she could grow up with a mother who modeled a confidence that comes from what is holy. So I opened up the Bible along with my heart and made a commitment to overcome. I went through a metamorphosis of spiritual renewal.

My friend Elisa is a life coach, and she says, "Real change happens when you start embracing fresh attitudes and focused habits, all in light of God's grace and truth. . . . Real life change is a process built on a partnership between you and God."[2]

So I started there, with a fresh attitude gleaned from Romans: "Do not be conformed to this age, but be transformed by the renewing of your mind" (12:2). This was the process of beginning my unmaking while embracing who I was created to be. I set out to renew my mind and restore my relationships. I practiced affirmation and reconciliation. I lived deep and wide. I discovered grace.

I thought that I couldn't be happy unless everyone else was happy with me, but I've learned that someone else's measure of satisfaction is not greater than God's portion of sanctification. It's not that life got easier. I still cried at rejection letters and felt left out when girlfriends got together without me. I still felt my heart shatter the day my daughter almost died and my husband went one way and I went another. I still sometimes scroll through social media and feel like I'm on the fringes.

It's just that now I'm fulfilled because I have found my portion.

So these days I don't turn my eyes downcast when I pass a mirror. I no longer hover by the nearest exit ready to make my escape from a crowded room. I fill my heart with songs of affirmation rather than refrains of self-loathing. I stopped hiding and started boldly living.

And my favorite shoes are a pair of dainty ballet slippers with silver sequins.

This is how I learned to flourish.

CHAPTER 1

Uninvited

We don't have a word for the opposite of loneliness,
but if we did, I could say that's what I want in life.
—Marina Keegan

This is a story all about how my life got flip-turned upside down.
No, wait, that's not me. That's the Fresh Prince of Bel-Air. Still, that's
an applicable assessment with a good beat, minus the whole "living in a
mansion in Bel-Air" part. Okay, and the prince part. Sadly, despite my
unrequited teenage love for Prince William, I am not royalty. Although
when I was catching up on today's news, the main headline was that Kate
Middleton wore the same outfit twice. I've basically been wearing the
same yoga pants and nursing tank since Saturday. I always knew I was
princess material.

The first thing I did when writing this book was ask my editor if it was
possible to include several photographs of myself. Not because I'm aspiring to a Kardashian level of selfies but because just about every picture of
me that was taken in my youth displays a level of awkwardness that must
be seen to be believed. I was an incredibly awkward adolescent. And I
don't mean awkward as in a Zooey Deschanel-esque "adorable" sort of
way. No. I mean a fairly gawky, "spent a lot of middle school trying to
avoid being shoved in a locker" awkward.

Unfortunately, though, it must be really expensive to print photographs in books or something. Obviously the solution to this problem is to

tell all your friends to buy *this* book, and then maybe it will be a best seller, and then we can sneak some pictures of "1988 Me" dressed as Cartoon Rockstar JEM into the next one. It will be worth it.

I spent most of my life wishing I were someone else. Someone prettier, braver, funnier. Someone who was lovable. Because stowed away in the depths of my heart was the belief that I was not. I've always felt unfinished, as though I'm perpetually in the process of becoming.

There is a lovely, oft-quoted sentiment by Marianne Williamson adorning many a Pinterest board that reads, "Our deepest fear is not that we are inadequate. Our deepest fear is that we are powerful beyond measure. It is our light, not our darkness that most frightens us."[1]

Nope.

That whole part about inadequacy? That is definitely my deepest fear, right after tornadoes and just before driving over large bodies of water. I'm not at all afraid of that powerful light she's talking about. Actually, I would really love to possess that light. I'd be all "hide it under a bushel? No, I'm gonna let it shine!"

No, my fear is the former—that I am inadequate. It's always been that one.

I thought growing up would provide me immunity against insecurity, but a few years ago I attended a conference and was chatting with some women afterwards when one of them put a finger to her chin and said, "I just can't figure out what it is about you." I felt flattered, like maybe I'd finally achieved a sort of alluring, mysterious charm. This was my moment. I was finally That Girl, and in a *good* way. Or at least that's what I thought until she continued with, "It's just like, you're so much better in writing."

Excuse me while I go put some salve on that burn.

If I hadn't already been insecure, that would have done it. At the start of the conference the organizer got up on stage and encouraged everyone to sit at a different table for each meal. "No saving seats for friends," she said. "It'll give us all a chance to mix and mingle and make new relationships." I was incredibly relieved because I'd gone to this writing conference knowing exactly no one, and so my very professional plan was *already* to be a table crasher. I was still incredibly nervous about sitting with strangers at every meal, but at least now I would look less like a weirdo and more like a girl who knew how to meticulously follow directions. Who doesn't want that in a new friend? It basically screams friend material.

At the next meal I put on my game face, which consisted of an extra layer of mascara and a permanent smile. I was going to look so friendly. People would totally want to be my friend. I walked up to a half empty table and gathered up all my courage to say an enthusiastic hello. "Sorry. These seats are saved," they responded curtly before turning back to their conversation. I stood rooted to the spot in a flustered state of embarrassment, partially because I was having junior high lunchroom flashbacks and partially because they were breaking the rules. I have a real affinity for rule following and fail to comprehend when people flagrantly break them. I stammered something awkward and went off in search of a more welcoming table that didn't invoke memories of standing alone with my lunch tray in a crowded middle school cafeteria.

What I wanted to do was rush back to the safety and seclusion of my hotel room. Seriously, every fiber in my body was shouting at me to make a mad dash out of there like that one scene from Forrest Gump when tiny Jenny is hollering at tiny Forrest to "Run, Forrest, run!" But then I saw they were serving triple chocolate cake for dessert and decided to take my chances. Because life is like a box of chocolates. You never know what you're going to get.[2]

(Plus, I paid a ton of money for that conference ticket. The least I could do was enjoy my cake.)

Eventually the woman explained that what she meant by "you're so much better in writing" was that I seemed more confident and self-assured in print, and she hadn't expected to find me so unsure of myself in person. To which I was like, "Of course I'm more confident in writing. In writing

I get a backspace key." I can rewrite a sentence over and over again until the words fall together with just the right cadence. Everything in text can be positioned and refined until it is polished. Unlike the other day when I felt really proud of myself for braving a trip to the grocery store with a new baby. I had on real clothes, I'd brushed my hair, and I finally felt like I had it all together. That is, until a sweet lady stopped to inform me that apparently when I put on my baby-wearing wrap, I had tied the back of my dress up in it, exposing my undergarments. And that is the story of how my first trip to the grocery store with two kids involved me flashing everyone on the way in. I am so good at motherhood. Also, I did not mean to take being naked and unashamed literally.

The conference wasn't my first time feeling excluded. There was the summer between elementary school and junior high, for example, when everything changed and I went from social to invisible. There was the day in eighth grade when none of my friends showed up to my party and then dumped me from our friend group, loudly and publicly in front of the lockers. There was the weekend of prom our senior year, when everyone paired off into couples and I was dressless and dateless. It was a succession of ordinary moments that created a cache of shame in me.

I spent much of my life on a quest to learn how to like myself. It was basically my holy grail. The most anyone ever offered me was a "fearfully and wonderfully made" or a "you are already enough." But those well-meaning words just fell into the chasm of my own self-deprecation. I didn't *feel* that way about myself so I didn't believe those things to be true. It was kind of like when your dad says you're beautiful and you think, "Yeah, you have to say that because you're my father. It's pretty much a basic requirement in your job description."

For me, the question was "How do I get from here to there?" From insecurity to confidence. From fear to freedom. From unbelief to belief.

I didn't just want to know it. I didn't just want to see the Bible verses printed on gold-rimmed paper but never feel them sparking to life within me. I wanted to be able to embrace it, believe it, and live it. I wanted a hallowed spirit of confidence to be my anthem. The problem was, after spending so many years feeling uncomfortable in my own skin, I didn't really know who I was. I had sort of pieced together a false personality based on attributes that people seemed to admire in my friends or what I thought was expected of me. I was just like Julia Roberts in *Runaway Bride*, except for that whole part where a bunch of hot guys wanted to marry me.

In an effort to leave my own island of insecurity, I began to collect other people's stories. I mean, I knew I had more issues than *Vogue* all on my own, but I wanted to know how we as women could encourage one another in an area in which we all share the same struggle. Over and over the women in my life expressed the desire to overcome their insecurity in favor of transparent and abiding love. I thought maybe we should all come together to conquer our secret fears.

And that's what brought me here. I'm pretty sure that's what brought *you* here too.

Almost everyone I spoke to while writing this book had an origin point for her insecurity. From a pointed comment about housework to a judgmental look from someone in the grocery store to an airbrushed advertisement in a magazine, the messages hurled at women were filled with insinuations about what we should be, rather than championing who we were created to be. I found that the catalyst for insecurity is almost always an interaction that leaves us feeling inadequate.

For me it started with an unfortunate school photo and a rainbow-striped sleeping bag.

CHAPTER 2

Rejected

I gave him my heart, and he took and pinched
it to death; and flung it back to me.
—Emily Brontë, *Wuthering Heights*

The first time I felt the sharp sting of rejection was when a long-time friend didn't invite me to her annual birthday sleepover. Every year since we were knee-high to a grasshopper had found us rolling out our sleeping bags on her living room floor. There were certain things I could count on in the spring: the metallic clanging of bats ringing in baseball season, the bright purple iris blossoms marching across our back fence, and choosing new pajamas to debut at the birthday sleepover.

I had felt the tension a little bit as she moved faster than me toward growing up. She was so much better at grasping the subtle changes that eluded me, but I never guessed this year would be the one in which I was conspicuously absent from her guest list. I found out on the bus ride home, when another girl chattered excitedly about the upcoming party, and I chimed in, assuming things hadn't changed. But they had. I sat in the awkward embarrassment of her dismissal long after they disembarked at their stop.

I felt humiliated, but mostly I felt unwanted.

So I did what any preteen girl would do. I stayed up late talking to my boyfriend about it. And by "boyfriend," I mean the picture of Jonathan Taylor Thomas that I tore out of *Teen Beat* magazine and taped above my bed. Admittedly it was a rather one-sided relationship, but I really felt as though his eyes conveyed a wisdom beyond his years. Sure, he didn't have any good advice for me, but he never failed to offer an encouraging smile. Also, I was eleven. My expectations for relationships weren't all that high. When my mother asked me when the party was going to be held, I lied and pretended there wasn't going to be a celebration that year. I was too ashamed to admit my own invitation wouldn't be arriving.

Twenty-odd years later I saw some photos on Facebook of my girlfriends enjoying a night out dancing, and I instantly felt excluded. *Why didn't they invite me?* I wondered, as old hurts rose to the surface and unbidden tears pricked my eyes. I went through all of the possible reasons in my head: I talk too much; I forgot to return that one girl's Tupperware for, like, a whole month; they don't actually like me and have just been pretending for all these years. I mulled over the pictures sullenly as I scrolled through my newsfeed in bed, where I'd been staying for the past two months on strict bed rest. Sure, the fact that I was on doctor-ordered bed rest and physically unable to leave my house is probably the most practical reason for why I wasn't invited to that particular outing, but try telling that to a hormonal pregnant girl with a history of feeling left out. My husband gave it a valiant effort but ended up just handing me a carton of rocky road ice cream and a spoon. (Admittedly, that did make me feel much better.)

Then I reread Mindy Kaling's book *Is Everyone Hanging Out Without Me?* because of solidarity. I was all, "That's a good question, Mindy. *Is* everyone hanging out without me? Because Facebook seems to think so."

As I was discussing this incident with a friend, she asked, "But would you have even wanted to go? Don't you pretty much hate dancing?" She was right, because going dancing is definitely not my scene. Once when my daughter Scarlette was about three years old, I was dancing around the kitchen in an attempt to be a Fun and Spontaneous Mom, when she suddenly stopped and cocked her head at me curiously.

"Um, Mommy? What are you trying to do with your body?"

"I'm dancing, Scarlette!"

She shook her head seriously and replied, "No, Mommy. Dat is NOT dancing."

From then on she always referred to my dancing in a voice that suggested she was using air quotes around the word—like, when I was brushing my teeth while whirling around the room to the Backstreet Boys one day, and Scarlette asked me for a drink of water. I told her to wait just a minute. "Mommy, dis is serious," she said. "Dis is no time for your 'dancing.'"

So dancing is not something I generally make a point of doing outside of my own home. But all of my insecurity meant I still wanted to be extended an invitation to go dancing, despite the fact that my girlfriends know my aversion to it. My desire to be included, to have the reassurance of belonging, means I always want an invitation.

(The exception to this rule is Candy Crush. I'm constantly being invited to play Candy Crush by random people on Facebook. It's like the universe is making up for all those years I wasn't invited to stuff by sending me an onslaught of unwanted Candy Crush invitations.)

This trait of needing to be included tends to manifest itself as being unreasonably needy, which is definitely the opposite of what people are looking for in healthy relationships. The experience of being excluded is such a painful one that sometimes we accumulate all our past rejections and project them onto our present circumstances. The small slight that we're currently agonizing over is magnified by the power of memory. It somehow soaks up all the spillover we never quite mopped up from earlier brush-offs. It becomes every rejection all over again, rolled into one.

In my insatiable desire for connection, I constantly felt hyperaware of any lack of it. If there was a circle forming somewhere, I wanted to be inside of it, but continuously felt as if I were on the periphery. It took a long time for me to realize that not being included in every activity on my friend's social calendars is not the same thing as being left out. This was an exhausting reality for both me to maintain and for my friends to endure, always needing reassurance of their acceptance.

Rejection is hard. Because regardless of our age, we all just want to fit in. Last year my daughter came home in tears when another little girl in her class told her she couldn't play with the rest of the girls because her shirt was ugly. Apparently cute peplum sweaters that your very stylish mother scored on clearance at Target were not *in* with the playground set. Shirts featuring Hello Kitty had apparently been deemed the attire of choice. With huge tears rolling down her cheeks, my four-year-old looked at me and sniffed, "She ran away from me and said I couldn't play with her because she didn't like my outfit. She said my outfit is not good.

"But maybe . . ." she said, "maybe if I get a better outfit, she can play with me tomorrow! Dat could be a great idea!" she said through her sniffles. We could buy a Hello Kitty shirt, she suggested. So that the other girls would like her.

I wanted to cry right alongside her.

Then we had a long talk about how she didn't need a better outfit for those girls to like her because we should not base our friendships on what people are wearing. We talked about how we should be nice to everyone. We talked about how hurtful it is to feel left out and how we should try hard not to make other people feel that way. It was a speech I was prepared not to need for a good five more years in the future. I didn't realize preschool politics would be so cutthroat.

"Do you understand what I'm saying, Scarlette?" I asked her, hopeful that the past nine-and-a-half minutes had penetrated her little heart with truth and love. She looked at me solemnly and replied, "Yes, Mommy, but I fink I need a chocowate chip gwanola bar now." So I think I definitely made an impression on her.

Being on the outside looking in is never the comfortable position. Lysa TerKeurst said, "Rejection isn't just an emotion we feel. It's a message that's sent to the core of who we are, causing us to believe lies about ourselves, others, and God. We connect an event from today to something harsh someone once said. That person's line becomes a label. The label becomes a lie. And the lie becomes a liability in how we think about ourselves and interact in every future relationship."[1]

Sounds accurate to me. And it sure doesn't sound like abundant life.

There will always be instances of exclusion in our lives. There will be the invitation that doesn't come in the mail, the pictures on Facebook we're absent from, the table we sit at alone. Those moments? They are never going to feel good. They are painful because they feel like a rejection of who we are as a person, leaving us exposed and raw and yearning. We think if we could just change who we are, then maybe those people will embrace us rather than exclude us.

Or at least that's what I thought until I moved to Canada.

On the first day of high school, I wore a pair of tight, flared pants with oversize wedge heels. I had learned my lesson about the whole footwear issue. The year was 1997, and I'd spent the entire summer perfecting my back-to-school outfit. After all, high school was going to be nothing like middle school. The awkwardness that had been my constant shadow for the past three years of junior high was over. This was going to be my fresh start. I stood with Laura Anne in the bustling hallway at the top of the stairs in the science building, taking it all in before heading to homeroom. I ran through my inner monologue, giving myself an encouraging pep talk. I pulled my shoulders back and raised my chin, ready to take on high school poised and assured and confident.

Then I promptly tripped and fell down the entire flight of stairs.

For most of my school years, I indulged in The Daydream. You know the one. The one where you start over somewhere in a completely new place where no one knows you, and you can assume an entirely new identity. Oh, y'all, I was so good in The Daydream. In The Daydream I had really shiny hair and I could do a toe touch. (Clearly I had very high aspirations as a child.) In The Daydream I was charming and self-assured. I never made awkward comments or fell down flights of stairs, and I always had the perfect, snappy comeback. Basically, I was Jessica Wakefield. (This is what happens when you spend your youth reading *Sweet Valley High* books.)

When I was twenty years old, I got to live out this little scenario when I moved to Vancouver, British Columbia. I mean, I still couldn't do a toe touch, but I figured I could reinvent myself. I realize moving to a different country by myself doesn't seem like something a person who struggles with confidence would do. That is an accurate observation. I did *not* plan to do that. I planned to move to Canada *with* someone, and at the last minute that someone changed her mind, leaving me to venture off to a foreign country on my own. I'm not bitter. Really it probably worked out for the best because I was moving to Canada as part of a work program with a mission group, and dependability is a trait you want in your missionaries. (Toe touches are negotiable in the mission field.)

This was my chance. I was literally moving across the country, from the Deep South to the West Coast and then crossing the border into Canada. I could be anyone I wanted.

I thought about faking a British accent, but then I worried I might meet my future husband on the trip and be forced to keep that up for the rest of my life. (Honestly, I still fail to see the flaws in that plan because I love a good British accent, but my best friends assure me it was a terrible idea.) As it happens, I didn't even need a faux British accent because in Canada I sound decidedly southern. In the South I only sound exceptionally southern when I spend a lot of time around my Tennessee family. Then I start adding a lot of extra syllables to words and saying things like "Y'all, I'm fixin' to git some cheese grits." The other reason I didn't need it was because of how anxious I ended up being about traveling to another country alone. By the time I reached the other side of the border, I was just so relieved to get through customs that I forgot about my plan to pretend to be someone else. That's right, I blew my one chance at fulfilling The Daydream. (You had one job, self!)

My main assignment that summer was to organize a community-wide youth sports camp for underprivileged kids. This was the perfect task for me given that I am incredibly uncoordinated and have never played a single team sport in my life. I'm not actually even sure how I got assigned the job, but I'm assuming that putting "Vice President of the Fellowship of Christian Athletes" on my internship application was probably a poor choice on my end. I can see how that might be misleading. Actually, I'm not sure how I got the FCA role either on account of how I never played any sports in high school. Probably I'm just very presidential.

I'm not even going to be modest: I killed it at that job. I organized that sports camp like a boss. Literally, because I was the boss of it. I cared so much about the success of that program, not because I felt like I had something to prove but because I wanted to create an impactful, meaningful experience for those kids.

It was then that I began to understand the work that God was cultivating in me.

I thought starting over with a new identity would be the thing that changed me from who I was into who I wanted to be. I thought I needed a clean slate and a fresh start so that I could rebuild myself from the ground up in order to ever make a difference in the world. What I found instead was that when I was unencumbered by the negative thoughts that I assumed people were having about me, I was free to delve into my gifts. I didn't need a newly constructed identity; I just needed to be free to be my best self. I had no idea my actual best self was so likable. My best self is funny and compassionate and . . . okay, my hair still tends to be frizzy, but I learned about straightening irons so that part is manageable.

For many years I let other people tell me who I was allowed to be. I built a tower out of their cutting words and snubs, and then I locked myself inside it like Rapunzel, minus the good hair. Much of the ammunition I gathered up to construct those walls came from what had been leveled at me during my youth, when I took the angst of my peers and decided it was the truth. Do you know what that means? It means I let someone else's adolescent assessment of me become my definition. But why? Why would I do that? I mean, there's a reason no one lets teenagers make important life decisions. Teenagers don't even have fully formed frontal lobes.

The other day, for instance, a friend told me that one of the teenage boys she teaches has a broken arm because he got in an argument with his girlfriend and jumped out of the car. While she was driving. Do you know why he did that? Because he's a teenager. Teenagers make stupid decisions. When I was a teenager, my friends and I once thought it would be a good idea to scale the gate of the golf course where our friend worked and drive the golf carts around. At night. In the dark. With no lights. After we left Wednesday night youth group. Not one of us thought this (possibly illegal) activity was a bad idea, except for me. Have I mentioned that I am a very strict rule follower? Unfortunately, I was also needy and easily susceptible to peer pressure, and so what I did was, I rode around in the golf cart while continuously reminding everyone that we were probably going to get arrested. I am a joy and delight to be around. It's really hard to see why I had trouble making friends.

The problem was that I had let myself be defined by other people. I had set my guidelines by other flawed humans rather than by the spirit of who I was created to be. Defining ourselves by the narrow perspective of another person limits us to only a small portion of our potential. It creates boundaries and restrictions where God intended for us to experience freedom. Seriously, that's not my opinion, that's in the actual Bible: "Where the Spirit of the Lord is, there is freedom" (2 Cor. 3:17).

Here's the thing: no one is allowed to tell you who you are. In a journey of self-discovery the only true author of your story is the one who spoke a universe into existence. The only words that truly define us are the red-letter ones, the capital letter Word who "became flesh and made his dwelling among us" (John 1:14 NIV). We will find ourselves by using the Word as a lamp unto our feet, letting it light our path. We just need to learn how to let it illuminate what God has already consecrated.

Consider this your formal invitation.

CHAPTER 3

Consumed

> The voice of Shame says, *I basically hate me; I need to get rid of me.* The voice of Discipline says, *I've got to fix me, because me is not good.* God says, *I love you; let me restore you.*
> —Stasi Eldredge

Transitioning from being an only child to being a big sister is a hard thing when you're five years old. We added a baby boy to our family, and this has been, shall I say, interesting. Partially because a new family member threw off the balance of our household, and partially because boys come with totally different equipment than I'm used to. I constantly forget to keep that little water pistol covered during diaper changes, is what I'm saying.

This has led to my normally happy little girl experiencing an onslaught of new and confusing emotions. She's feeling understandably left out and disconcerted by the upheaval in our family routines. I'm not sure she realized the extent to which she would need to be sharing my attention and affections. After yet another bedtime interruption from a crying baby brother, she said to me, "Um, Mommy? I fink maybe we should give baby Ridley back to his real mommy now." When I told her that I was, in fact, Ridley's real mommy, which meant I was both her mommy and his mommy, Scarlette threw her hands in the air and yelled, "What? Are you KIDDING me about dis?"

The other day we found ourselves embroiled again in an emotional meltdown of epic proportions that was the result of her feeling unfavored.

In my five years of mothering her, I had never seen her lash out this way, raw and aching. Her tantrum was such that my husband had to carry her out of the car, all limbs flailing and red-faced. "I don't want to be so sad! Please don't let me do this to myself!" she cried, gasping for breath between sobs. She repeated it over and over with her head on her daddy's shoulder, tears streaming down her cheeks and tiny fists railing against his chest.

As I watched my husband try to console her, I saw a physical imitation of all my own inner turmoil.

The other day I saw a trailer for a movie, one of those annoying video ads that flitted across my computer screen. Normally I would press the upper right hand corner X, but this time I clicked my mouse on the play button because I caught sight of Ewan McGregor, and everyone's day can be made better with an infusion of Ewan McGregor in it, that's what I always say. As the video began to play, I saw that he was dressed as Jesus. It soon became apparent that the scene playing out on the screen was a filmmaker's version of when Jesus was alone in the desert, spending forty days locked in a battle with Satan.

This passage of the Bible has always been one that felt elusive to me. (See the Gospel accounts of Matthew, Mark, and Luke.[1]) It was so hard for me to comprehend that Jesus would actually struggle with the temptations that Satan presented Him with, on account of how He was Jesus and all. How much could Satan really torment the Son of God, I wondered. So I wasn't too vested in this video except that, well, have you ever seen Ewan McGregor?

But then the camera came to rest on Satan, and we see the enemy for the very first time. It is Ewan McGregor dressed as Jesus, a mirror image. And through the artistry of cinema, this scene became intensely real to me, in at least this one aspect, because it's a struggle I understand: I am my very own worst enemy.

Curt Thompson, author of *The Soul of Shame*, writes, "The reality is that most shame takes place inside your head dozens of times every day. It's silent, subtle, and characterized by the quiet self-condemning conversation that we've learned since we were kids."[2]

We are caught in a cycle of shame that poisons us from the inside out.

One of the proverbs says, "The words of the reckless pierce like swords" (Prov. 12:18 NIV), and it's me who is reckless, destructive with my own inner voice. I question my every decision, I belittle my own character, I fling pointed accusations at myself. My best weapon is self-deprecation, and I wield it well. I fill my bow with pointed arrows and I aim them at my own heart.

This is the way we are defeated, with our own words, at our own hands.

My daughter has to do occupational therapy to help strengthen her wrists. She was born with her bones broken, and she's never been able to make them work quite the way they're supposed to. At five years old she struggles heavily with fine motor skills, frustrated that she can't catch her own zipper or slip a button through a buttonhole. Her peers can do it, and so she keeps trying because she wants to be on par with them, independent and shrugging off the teacher's help when she needs to slip on a jacket to play outside. We practice writing her name over and over and over again, but her movements are jerky. Her wrists just can't catch the motion. She puts her head down on the desk teary-eyed and tells me her classmates made fun of her handwriting. "They said I write like a baby," she tells me softly before slamming her pencil down in frustration. "I'm no good at this. I'm just no good." The sense of shame rolls off of her in waves, and I buoy her before she can drown herself in it.

It doesn't matter whether or not she can write. It doesn't matter if she still needs a straw cup because she can't bend her wrists in a backward motion or if she fumbles with the snaps on her shorts. It only matters what she tells herself when she's hurting.

We regularly sing a little jingle in our house that goes "Just keep trying, you'll get better!" Feel free to add this to your parenting repertoire. I stole it from Daniel Tiger's mom because that woman is an excellent parental role model. She has an extraordinary amount of patience for a predator. Plus, she's full of helpful advice, like, "When you have to go potty, STOP and go right away!" Sure, she's an animated character on a PBS show, but I'll take good parenting advice anywhere I can get it.

I try to encourage my daughter not to wallow in negative self-talk. When she says, "I'm no good at writing," I say, "Writing is hard for you. You're good at lots of things. I'm proud of you for showing a spirit of perseverance." Then she asks me what perseverance means because she's five.

The point is, my words to her are largely encouraging and full of hopeful possibility because I want to give her a well of truth to draw from. I had let my own reservoir run dry until I was so parched that any affirmation felt like a quenching for my thirst, and I drank it in greedily. I don't want her reaching for that cup because I want her to know she already has her portion. "The LORD is my portion," says my soul, "therefore I will put my hope in him" (Lam. 3:24).

Here is what we are going to do, you and I and Scarlette. We are going to rewrite this narrative. We are going to take up what God says about us as an anthem because "what you say about yourself means nothing in God's work. It's what God says about you that makes the difference" (2 Cor. 10:17–18 MSG). We are going to reclaim the portion that is our inheritance. We are going to do this because the things that God says about us are so much better than the things we say to ourselves.

I am a place where God's Spirit lives. (1 Cor. 6:19)

I am God's incredible work of art. (Eph. 2:10)

I am a whole new person with a whole new life. (2 Cor. 5:17)

I am accepted. (Rom. 15:7)

I am greatly loved. (Rom. 5:8)[3]

I talk to my daughter this way because I want her inner monologue to be different than mine. I want what she says about herself to be what God says about her. I want her to hear that she has worth.

I want the same for you.

Ephesians 4:29 says, "No foul language should come from your mouth, but only what is good for building up someone in need, so that it gives grace to those who hear," and that doesn't just apply to how we speak to others. It's an edict for how we speak to ourselves as well. Only what is good. Replacing our inner critic with words that speak truth and life is the first step to overcoming our insecurity.

Listen to what God says about us, about you, and put that refrain on repeat like a record until it becomes your heart song.

———⚓

Scarlette does this thing where when she gets mad at me, she goes into her room, lines up all her stuffed animals across the foot of her bed, and then plops herself down in the center of it and airs all her grievances to them. Not only is this exceptionally cute, it is also saving me a ton of money on therapy. Those stuffed My Little Ponies were an excellent investment. She gets herself quite worked up during these tirades because her emotional level is always set at one hundred. Most of the time this means she is exuberantly happy, like a chipper little pixie, but on the rare occasions in which she is sad or angry, she cannot contain the intensity of her emotions.

The one thing Scarlette wants more than anything in the world is for me to sleep in her bed with her. This is the pinnacle of fun for Scarlette, mostly because she's not the one fending off a foot to the face all night. Sharing a bed with Scarlette is like trying to sleep while the

U.S. gymnastics team practices their floor routine on your mattress. So when she discovered that her new baby brother was going to sleep in our bedroom, she was gravely offended and convened her tribal council of stuffed companions to bare her soul to. Hearing her so distraught, I decided to step up and do the responsible, parental thing. I stood outside her door and eavesdropped on her sob session.

It was so funny, I wrote it down verbatim. This is how it went:

Mommy never lets me choose anything! It make-ed me so sad! I don't want my books to get dirty! I just want Mommy to have a sleepover with me! I don't have anyone to sleep with! Mommy only sleeps with Daddy, and I don't want to sleep alone! I hate the color purple! I'm too little to go through this!

That is not even the slightest bit embellished. I really enjoy how she expresses her feelings about the situation at hand and then goes on to give voice to every frustration her little heart feels. For instance, I also do not want my books to get dirty, and I do not particularly care for the color purple. Those things have nothing to do with me not letting her sleep in my bed while I'm nursing an infant, but I enjoy knowing she feels that way.

Since her baby brother was born, these little outbursts have been a more frequent occurrence. The other day I was juggling both the baby and the breast pump when Scarlette asked me to look at her painting. The only problem was that I had set her easel up on the front porch because I'm a southern girl, and in the South the best way to clean your child after letting them paint is to just hose them down on the front lawn. I didn't particularly think my neighbors would care to see me half-dressed, so I asked her to give me just a minute to finish what I was doing. She tilted her little face down, drooped her shoulders wearily, and said sadly, "Yeah. Because babies are more better than big sisters, right?" Then it took me even longer to peek at her artwork on account of how I was busy pulling the dagger out of my heart.

One morning as we were getting ready for preschool, Scarlette held up a shirt that she had dug out of the laundry basket, and said, "Mommy, I wish I could just wear dis shirt to school today so dat everybody would think dat I look SO cute."

"Well, we can't wear that one today because it's kind of dirty," I told her, "but we can wear it another time after I wash it. I bet everyone will think you look cute in your other shirt, though."

After a few minutes of Scarlette insisting that no one would think she looked cute in the clean shirt, I said, "Yes, they will. Trust me." Then Scarlette looked at me for a long minute, shook her head, and in a totally deadpan voice replied, "Nope. I don't trust you. I just trust dis shirt."

I get it, because assimilation is so much easier than self-acceptance. Fitting in is easier than standing out. We can become so obsessed with fitting the mold that we forget our blueprint, the one that was intricately designed with our uniqueness in mind. In our quest for sameness we overlook the imprint of Ephesians on our souls.

My heart breaks for my daughter as we work through all of her big feelings because I understand what it's like to think you know who you are, and then all of a sudden find yourself struggling to figure out where you fit.

CHAPTER 4

Squad Goals

Raise your hand if you've ever been personally
victimized by Regina George?
—Janice Ian, *Mean Girls*

Most of my childhood was spent on a blue-and-white striped swing set on the top of the hill in our backyard where I would simultaneously swing my legs and lift my voice as high as they both could go. With a Walkman on my hip and headphones on my ears, I would serenade the neighborhood with a carefully curated selection of songs on my mix tape from dawn till dusk. (Partially because in the nineties our parents sort of locked us outside and told us to have fun and drink from the garden hose if we were thirsty, so I didn't have a lot of options.) I imagined that I was a contestant on *Star Search*, dazzling host Ed McMahon with my jazzy rendition of "Hangin' Tough" or my melodic arrangement of "A Whole New World." I legitimately believed I would one day be discovered by someone passing by, hearing my sparkling soprano belting out the chorus of Reba McEntire's "Fancy."

I'm sure the neighbors thought I was just a little treasure.

I loved to sing. I stood in the front row of the school chorus every year, mostly because the front row is where they put the very short people, and I auditioned for every solo. The first day, when the girl who sat behind me in my seventh grade chorus class taunted me, I was bewildered. The second day, when the girls who I thought were my friends joined in, I was brokenhearted and dismayed by the betrayal. The third day, when she physically assaulted me while the teacher was out of the room, I was panic-stricken. By the end of the week, I was physically ill at the thought of going to school.

My parents had always told me to hit back, but at four-and-a-half feet tall, I was tiny and timid in the face of my bully. I wouldn't have even known where to land the blow. The second time she shoved me to the floor, I wiped the blood from my lip. I was such a wisp of a girl.

I decided to be invisible.

That day I walked the quarter mile home from the bus stop slowly, lingering so the tears wouldn't appear so fresh on my cheeks when I reached my front door. In the distance a semi-truck rumbled toward me, and for a split second I thought, "I could just step off this curb and all of this pain would end." I stood staring hollow and cold and felt the wind blow heavy as it passed. I looked both ways before I crossed the street, walking down the long, winding driveway and past the twisted flowering branches of a gnarled dogwood tree. I thought about the drawer full of sharp metal in the kitchen and the way it might feel to put steel to skin. I thought about the quickness of cutting yourself right out of existence and how life could drain from your veins long after it was smothered out in your heart.

I was thirteen years old.

I only thought about it, but I felt like I was already disappearing.

My social circle occasionally overlaps with a woman who has this way of always making me feel like an outsider. I think it's her tone, or the way she makes subtle comments as though she wants to be sure I know my place in the hierarchy we share with a mutual friend. But mostly it's because she does the same thing each and every time I interact with her: she pretends she doesn't remember me.

I'm pretty sure it's an act because, while she could potentially be suffering from a case of Dory-like forgetfulness, I once co-babysat her kid for an afternoon, so I'm fairly confident she knows who I am. I mean, otherwise the problem here is her propensity for leaving her kids with total strangers. Despite this, she repeatedly makes comments each time she sees me, such as, "Oh, right, aren't you so-and-so's friend?" Or else she introduces herself to me as though we've never met before. I always make polite conversation, but in my head I'm all, *Remember that time I wiped your child's bottom? YOU KNOW ME.*

For a long time I couldn't figure out why I so intensely, viscerally disliked having to interact with her. I thought maybe it was because I found her *Finding Nemo* shtick highly annoying. But the truth is, it's because she plays on my deepest fear: that I am so insignificant I am completely forgettable. It makes me feel small and less-than, like everything about myself is pulling inward. It makes me feel as though I'm not even worth the time and effort of remembering. It makes me feel invisible.

It makes me feel like that day I walked home alone from the bus stop when I was thirteen years old.

One of the worst feelings in the world is to not be seen. No one wants to go through life unnoticed. We all just want someone to tell us we matter. During college I worked at a coffee shop. I loved that job because I love caramel Frappuccinos and I love talking to strangers. I have a remarkable memory, in that I can remember entire paragraphs of books I read when I was nine or the name of a person I met briefly in line at the grocery store three years ago, and yet I perpetually have no idea where I last left my car keys. (Much to my husband's chagrin, the answer is never "On the little hook he installed specifically for me to place my keys on.")

I'm also naturally chatty, so I made a point of striking up conversations with customers as I made their drinks. I learned a lot about our regulars and would file certain bits of information away to revisit later, asking them about their lives when they came in for a cappuccino. My coworkers teased me about this, and I used to brush it off by declaring that it earned me more tips. But the truth is, I worked the five a.m. shift, and there is just something special about starting off someone's day with kindness. For every person that I asked how his or her kids liked dance class or wished good luck on their exam or slid extra biscotti in their bag during a tough divorce, I was saying, "I see you."

This is why those "Dear Mom" open letters go viral on the Internet. They overtake my newsfeed as person after person clicks "like" because those words are validation: you are not alone, you are seen. Whenever my husband and I feel distant from one another, it's usually because one of us doesn't feel seen or heard. That doesn't mean a lot of words weren't said. Usually a lot of words *have* been said. Mostly by me.

All we ever want is to be seen.

Social media sometimes gets a pretty bad reputation, but it has really deepened my prayer life. Seriously, every single day when I log on to Instagram and scroll through my feed, I put my hand to my heart and think, "Dear Lord, thank You that social media did not exist when I was in my adolescent years." I once auditioned for *The Real World*. And while I didn't make it past the second round of auditions, I consider it the Lord's great anointing on my life that eighteen-year-old me was not broadcast on MTV and forever immortalized on YouTube.

What I did have to document my youth was a diary. In fact, I have a box full of old ones because my childhood self thought it would be a good idea to save them all for my future children to read. It seemed a very romantic notion at the time as I pictured my eventual offspring poring over my deepest thoughts and gleaning bits of wisdom from the pages. Then I reread those diaries as an adult and realized no one should be subjected to that level of teenage angst.

Dear Diary,

I am going out with Michael. I really am. Today, Katie leaned over and said, "Michael, are you going out with Kayla?" And he said YES. I love Michael!

More disturbing than the fact that I apparently let my romantic fate be decided by whoever wanted to call me their girlfriend at the time was the very next page:

Dear Diary,

I hate Michael!

I was like a little modern-day Jane Austen. My diary was pretty much the same plot as her book *Emma*, "I love John! I hate John!"

By the time I hit junior high, I also wrote a lot of diatribes about the It Girls. It is such a movie cliché, the table full of popular girls in a school cafeteria. I suppose it's because of how art imitates life, and it certainly captures mine: cinder block walls and checkerboard floors and intangible walls around certain sections. One table was all baby doll dresses and knee socks, and when I tried to sit there with old friends, I was shunned. They were in, I was out. Their opinion meant everything to me only because it meant everything to everyone else. I didn't even particularly like them, but their approval was the only way to ensure that everyone else liked me. And as a teenager, nothing felt more important than that.

My youth pastor tried to prep us for peer pressure by having us memorize Romans 8:31: "If God is for us, who can be against us?" (NIV). But I was just hitting my tweenage years, so I was like, "The girls sitting at the popular table. They are most definitely against me." I'm just saying that I wouldn't have begrudged God a good Old Testament smiting.

I thought when I grew up, I would outgrow the notion of It Girls, but instead it seems society decided to make the very concept of It Girls an even more pervasive thing as I matured. Before social media, celebrity seemed at a distance, mostly flashbulbs and magazine features. Now our culture is obsessed with consuming celebrity, and our access seems unfettered. All it takes is installing an app on your cell phone, and suddenly Instagram lets you peek into the intimate lives of movie stars and musicians. It seems exclusive in a different way, like front-row seats to something unattainable.

It's easy to feel insignificant when the rest of the world looks picture-perfect in the palm of your hand. Whether it's Facebook statuses of a friend's family in matching first-day-of-school outfits while you're in yesterday's sweats and running late for drop-off, or Instagram pics of Taylor Swift surrounded by supermodels and hashtagged "squad goals," these quick glimpses into someone else's life can make our own lives pale by comparison. They can also make us question our place in our friendships. Are we in or out? Are we part of the tribe?

I blame Taylor Swift for the introduction of squad goals into the current vernacular. (I blame her for a lot of things actually, like my penchant for skinny jeans and red lipstick.) Personally, my #squadgoals would consist of the members of The Baby-Sitter's Club or the cast of *Hart of Dixie*. I presume the fact that my ideal squad is made up of entirely fictional characters is quite telling of my level of coolness.

But mostly, I think squad goals, for any of us, are indicative of our desire to belong. To fit and to fit in.

I was scheduled to speak at an event about my book, so I parlayed the travel into a road trip with one of my girlfriends, Jess. We stopped at a trendy restaurant in downtown Nashville and talked about fitting in as an adult. "I'm so intimidated by this group of women at our church," she told me. "They just all seem so perfect." She scrolled through her newsfeed and then flashed me a photo of a group of women laughing in front of an exposed brick wall. "See? Total squad goals," she sighed.

The trip had fallen early in my second pregnancy, when I was in the throes of morning sickness. I had spent the morning revisiting my breakfast before attempting to give my ashen face some semblance of color. Even if I had been at the top of my sartorial game, it wouldn't have mattered. I entered the auditorium and was immediately intimidated by the room full of stylish women, almost in uniform: black-and-white striped shirt, green utility vest, skinny jeans, ankle boots. I looked down at my coral pink eyelet top that I scored for three dollars at a consignment sale, and it was like the chunky-heeled shoe incident all over again.

"Total squad goals," I side-whispered to Jess.

I couldn't help but feel slightly out of sync. I mean, on the one hand, I was in the middle of my biggest dream, something I had worked so hard toward. I was the headliner for that event, and I still felt insecure, out of place, and small by comparison. That day I learned that you can watch your dreams come true and still feel a longing. You can be in the spotlight and still feel invisible.

I am grateful for the infinite nature of grace because I'm still in the process of overcoming.

———✦

Scarlette and I were driving home from the store the other day when she got all bent out of shape because I wouldn't replay the song we'd just listened to. I tried to no avail to explain to a five-year-old the radio doesn't work like that, but she's been raised in the era of the iPod and can't grasp such a concept. Through her tears she lashed out at me, and for the first time she said accusingly, "You can't be my best friend anymore!" I explained to her that while it was okay for her to feel sad and even be upset with me, those words were a very hurtful thing to say to someone.

And then I thought about the sixth grade.

I sat in study hall, sifted into the cafeteria with the other kids who arrived to school before the first bell, and worked quietly on artfully arranging the glitter section of my sticker book. Sticker books were all the rage in *fifth grade*, and my collection of hologram Sanrio sets had been cause for great jealousy on the playground. In sixth grade, however, stickers books were totally passé. They went from being the hottest thing to babyish in the short span of a single summer—yet another growing-up event on which I did not get the memo.

Imagine my surprise, then, when the pretty, popular girl from my third-period class slid into the seat next to me. Rarely did anyone sit with me in the mornings.

She struck up a conversation and asked casually if I'd finished our math homework, wondering aloud if she could see it because she'd forgotten hers. I started to say no, but loneliness caused the word to leave my lips as a yes. I opened my notebook and let her copy it. She even walked with me to gym class after math that day.

The following morning was the same. I slid my paper across the table, trading my hesitancy about the cheating for the satisfaction of friendship. For the next couple of weeks I basked in being on the edge of her spotlight as we walked through the locker-filled halls. People talked to us, people talked to me when I was with her, and I thought it might tip me over the threshold of acceptance. I was sure my terrible junior high experience was turning around . . . until the day she mockingly told my secret crush that I liked him, laughing at my mortification as I blushed furiously in the seat next to him.

"How could you do that?" I whispered as I followed her out of class. "I thought we were friends!"

She spun around and looked at me with disdain. "We're not friends," she hissed. "You mean nothing to me." And then she walked off to gym, leaving me standing alone, not only in the middle of the hallway but also of one of life's greatest lessons.

She never spoke to me again.

(The joke's on her. I'm really terrible at math.)

I desperately wanted her to like me for more than my math homework, and so I'd spilled my secrets to her, thinking that making her my confidant would create the closeness I was craving. Pro tip: this is a terrible tactic for any relationship. You'd think I'd have learned from this and not made the same mistake twice, but instead it became my guiding strategy in my early dating years. I was all "Hi, nice to meet you, here's a bunch of emotional information about me, and now I am way more invested in this relationship than you are!" I'm sure this was not at all frightening for teenage boys. I have no idea why so many guys broke up with me under the guise that I was too "needy." What a line that was.

Or, okay, completely on target and disturbingly accurate. Whatever.

CHAPTER 5

Making Out

> "Oh," said Ron, his smile faded slightly. "Are you that bad
> at kissing?" "Dunno," said Harry, who hadn't considered
> this, and immediately felt rather worried. "Maybe I am."
> J. K. Rowling, *Harry Potter and the Order of the Phoenix*

On Wednesday morning the sun hovered just over the
horizon as I sipped the first cup of coffee and pondered the question that
had been plaguing me since I awoke. "What in the world was I going to
do with Scarlette?"

I realize this seems trivial, but she had spent the previous day scaling
the walls. I mean that literally, on account of how she had shimmied up a
door frame. I was perfectly happy to let her amuse herself this way, except
that I had a deadline to meet, and Scarlette clinging on to my office door
frame was not going to help that happen.

So I did what any mom in my situation would do. I packed her into
the car and drove to Chick-Fil-A, where they have free Wi-Fi, large
vanilla iced coffees, and a glass-walled playground. I'm not saying I caged
my child in at a fast-food facility in order to get a little bit of time for
myself, but I'm not saying I didn't either.

Our server was a friendly teenage boy wearing a crisp pink bow tie
and a contagious smile that he kept flashing at Scarlette. (I'm guessing
this may have been because she dressed herself that day and was wearing a
snail headband with large, light-up antenna eyeballs.) I could tell she was

taken with him because she kept trying to catch his eye and then would giggle hysterically every time he played peekaboo with her.

There were no other children for her to play with because of the early hour, so I figured she just had a healthy appreciation for his attentiveness. And honestly, I could see why she felt that way. When she knocked over my entire drink and he appeared at the table like magic with extra napkins and a new cup of coffee, I thought I just might marry him myself. But later as he walked past us carrying a tray, she cocked her head to the side coquettishly, pursed her lips, and said, "Hey. You're my boyfriend. Yeah. My BOYFRIEND. You're my FIRST boyfriend." Before I even had a chance to react to this pronouncement, she gazed up at him, smiled sweetly, and asked, "So. Do you fink you can handle dat?"

I don't even know where she learned about boyfriends, except that she did ask if she could get married after her beloved Sunday school teacher's recent wedding. So basically, I blame the church.

When we finally pushed our way through the double doors at Chick-Fil-A on our way out, she glanced up at me with her precocious little smile and said, "So Mommy. I made my first BOYFRIEND today. What do you fink about dat?"[1]

I thought she might just be a handful in her teenage years, is what I thought about that.

I also thought about my own dating life and the way it shaped me. Unlike my little early bloomer, I was sixteen when I met the boy who would be my first love. He had sandy blonde hair that fell over one eye like Jordan Catalano and a wide smile that lit me up from the inside whenever he turned it my direction. He kissed me as the sun set over the beach, the first time anyone had ever pressed their lips to mine, and I thought that all the love in all the world was right there between us as the waves lapped at our feet. It was the quintessential storybook romance, and I let myself be swept away.

The summer I fell in love for the first time was the same one in which my parents' marriage was unraveling. We did not even see it coming, my sister and I. They hid the cracks well until it erupted around us, angry and swift. So I escaped into this new relationship, filled with the wonder of young love. He made me feel special; I felt lucky that he chose me. It was beyond all of my own expectations. I took shelter in the way he held my hand and how he would pick me up and reenact that one scene from the movie *Armageddon* while singing Aerosmith's "I Don't Want to Miss a Thing." I didn't want to miss a thing. I wanted to escape the fighting and the fractured family life.

So all the love was draining out of our home at the same time a boy first said those three little words to me. That same summer the divorce was final. My dad moved out. My mother's volatile boyfriend moved in.

And then the boy I loved sat in the backseat of his family's station wagon and drove off to Michigan.

In the words of Dickens, "It was the best of times, it was the worst of times." It made love confusing. It felt dangerous and alluring at the same time. I was desperate for it and dismayed by it.

It may be why my dating life went a little off the rails.

My best friend, Tiffani, is beautiful. Not in a "beauty is in the eye of the beholder" and I'm biased because I'm her BFF sort of way. No, she is legitimately beautiful in a prom queen and random people constantly stopping to tell her she looks like Cameron Diaz sort of way. She's also incredibly sweet and kind and also shy, and hates when people talk about her looks, so she'll be a little bit mortified to read this paragraph. Unfortunately for her, writing is my only talent. I've got to cash in where I can.

The thing that happens when you are a beautiful girl who is also evangelical is that apparently God tells many, many boys they're supposed to marry you. I know this because of the sheer number of boys who've told my best friend that God told them they were supposed to marry her as though they were on some celestial version of *The Bachelorette*. Most of them explained that it was her pure heart and love for the Lord that attracted them, and that they were sure God had designed her to be their helpmate. She does have a beautifully pure heart and love for the Lord. (And also, there's the looks-just-like-Cameron-Diaz thing.)

Several of my girlfriends had a similar experience. One day a friend was sitting alone in her dorm room when she heard a knock on the door. So she answered it because, you know, Jesus says, "Behold, I stand at the door and knock." That's when she found a stranger on the other side of the door, only it wasn't so much Jesus as it was some guy she'd never met before, who'd looked her up in the college directory and showed up at her dorm room to tell her that God had told him she was the girl he was supposed to marry. So it did turn out to be a sort of spiritual experience after all, except replace the world "spiritual" with "stalkerish."

After a third guy declared God's intentions for *another* one of my friends to be his bride, she started work on a rejection speech (for future such occurrences) that mentioned how God had decidedly not said the same thing to her. Rarely did the guys accept my friend's word on this. They just kept insisting my friends pray about it which, ironically, is incredibly insulting to the woman you claim you want to marry because of her "deep relationship with God."

For my part, not a single boy ever told me that God had proclaimed he should marry me. My best guess is that when you're working with bad hair and a rough bout of acne, maybe those boys spend a little bit more time laying out a fleece, like in the story of Gideon from the Bible. Mostly what guys said to me was, "Kayla, I just love your pure heart and love for the Lord, and so I know I can trust you with this: Can you set me up with your best friend?" (I'm not bitter.)

You think I'm exaggerating, likely because I am admittedly prone to the dramatics, but I assure you I am not. Tiffani and I went to a tiny, private college, and as such there were exactly eight guys on campus that we swooned over from afar, all upperclassmen. One of those guys, who had eyes as clear blue as the Caribbean, happened to be in our Ethics class, which meant Ethics was the only class we faithfully attended. That's where we learned he worked in the mailroom, and so after that we stopped by said mailroom every single day, despite the fact that in an entire semester we had received approximately one piece of mail. We took to calling him Ethical Nick.

One day he caught up with us outside of the mailroom, which was the first time he'd ever spoken to us outside of our daily faux mail check-ins. He didn't even bother making small talk. He just straight up asked Tiffani to the upcoming frat formal. She politely, although slightly reluctantly, declined on account of the fact that she had a boyfriend. But as we turned to leave, he put a hand on my shoulder and said, "So you were, like, my second choice. Do you want to go?"

Here's a life lesson for all three of the men reading this book: Never tell a girl she was your second choice. Especially if your first choice was her gorgeous best friend that you just asked out literally right in front of her. It's like he learned nothing in that Ethics class. Even then, at the epitome of my confidence issues, I was offended enough to turn him down flat. Just kidding, I totally considered it for a moment due to the combination of low-self esteem and how incredibly physically attractive he was. I might have even answered yes if Tiff hadn't been sending me not-so-subtle signals by tilting her head frantically and wiggling her eyebrows. The fact that I managed to say no remains one of my proudest moments.

(I cannot stress enough just how blue his eyes were, y'all.)

I spent two years in a relationship that I thought was heading straight to the altar. I thought this mostly because what my church taught about dating was that I should only date to get married, not because I thought we would make compatible life partners. I just really wanted to date him, and so I figured that since he wanted to date me too, it was surely a sign from above that we were supposed to get married. Obviously this was a solid, well-thought-out life plan. There was also the part about how he told me he wanted to marry me and took me to look at engagement rings, so you can see how I might have assumed we would definitely be getting hitched.

After it crashed and burned, however, I decided to just say yes to every single person who asked me on a date. Not that this happened with any great frequency, but I was devastated by the breakup. I thought it meant I was easy to discard. I assumed if that person no longer wanted me, then I must be undesirable, and thus it would be really hard to find someone who would want to marry me.

Shockingly, this experiment led to a bunch of horrible dates. Like the one where I went on a date with a guy a few years older than me who frequented the coffee shop where I worked. He spent the entire evening calling me "kiddo." Then there was the guy who stared at me over dinner and kept making comments about how much I looked like his ex-girlfriend. Which is totally what you want to hear on your first date. I went on a few dates with a guy who was very into cars. I was not very into cars, but I read a few issues of *Car and Driver* and then pretended I was. It was on the third date that he drove to a parking lot full of car enthusiasts and asked me to stand by the car and look pretty. It was like something out of *The Fast and the Furious*. I lasted three more dates after that.

A guy I worked with asked me to go to a fireworks display with him. I didn't think this was a date because I never assumed I was being asked on a date unless someone very clearly declared, "The time we'll be spending together is a date." It wasn't until we hopped in the back of the truck to watch the fireworks that I noticed he had a mattress in the truck bed. I realize I was needy, but if I were going to put out, it would not be in the back of a truck in the middle of the Fourth of July picnic. (You're welcome, Dad.)

The whole problem with this plan was that it just perpetuated my belief that I was expendable. Each new rejection felt like an affirmation that I was fundamentally flawed. I could have gone on a thousand dates, but I would still have felt unwanted because the problem wasn't a lack of romance or love. It was that I didn't love myself. I kept searching for another half when what I needed was to be whole.

(Except for the guy who dumped me for not wanting to share his fork over dessert when I had my own perfectly good set of utensils. Even at my most desperate, I knew with a deep and blessed assurance I did not want to spend my life eating off a fork that had someone else's cheesecake skid marks on it.)

The most telling romantic interlude, however, was The Older Guy. The one I didn't have any romantic feelings for but decided to date anyhow because it made me feel mature and important. He liked to take me out for sushi and to the symphony, and I put on fancy heels and tried to make it fit, even though I'm more of a karaoke kind of girl. But I thought, *You know, I should be someone who likes sushi and the symphony*. This sounded like a way better version of myself, except for the part about how it involved eating raw fish. That's how afraid I was that no one would want me. I just kept smiling over raw fish as I inwardly gagged my way through dinner.

So my backup plan was to become a missionary. Go big or go home, that's my motto. Or rather, go very far from home because no one questions why girls of marriageable age serving in the mission field do not have a significant other. I figured it would just look like I was really spiritual and sacrificial and not as though no one wanted me. I think it's obvious that my heart was in entirely the right place. Except the opposite of that.

/

CHAPTER 6

Between the Sheets

Reader, I married him.
—Charlotte Brontë, *Jane Eyre*

I first learned about sex when I was five years old. My mother was pregnant with my younger sister and explained the basics to me when I asked how, exactly, that baby got in her tummy. Horrified at the idea that someday someone might have to see me naked, I declared I would never, EVER engage in this activity. And then I promptly forgot about all of it until I was around twelve years old.

My mother got off lucky, if you ask me. Scarlette was also five years old when I discovered I was pregnant again, and she did not dismiss the topic so easily. Unlike my mother before me, I did not tell my daughter what sex is. Mostly on account of how Scarlette repeats everything she hears and often blurts out things that make for slightly inappropriate conversation with strangers at the grocery store. Like this one time when she told the teenage boy bagging our groceries that her mommy wasn't wearing any undergarments. What she meant was that I was not wearing training pant Underoos like the ones we were purchasing for her, but she was three years old and not so good with the syntax, resulting in more awkward moments like this than I can count.

(Another time she confidently introduced me as her "Sister-Mommy," which left me hastily explaining to a random cashier that I am not, in fact, a polygamist. I was just as confused about it as you are.)

So when Scarlette asked me how the baby got in my tummy, I did what any responsible, wise parent would do.

I panicked.

And told her it was magic.

"Oh, you mean growed-up magic?" she asked, cocking her head to the side knowingly.

"Um, sure. Grownup magic." That seemed totally innocent. No way was that coming back to bite me.

Right. Later that day she looked at the lady slicing up our lunch meat at the deli and said delightedly, "Guess what! My Mommy has a baby in her tummy! Do you know how it got in there? My daddy and mommy put it in there with growed-up magic!"

I wasn't very far into my seventh grade year when the "magic" topic of sex came around again. I was sitting with two girls I'd known since kindergarten on the bus ride home. That day their conversation was about how far one of them had gone with her boyfriend, who was a grade above us, and how pressured my friend felt to do more. Their conversation shocked me. It also shocked my mother later that night when I tentatively asked her what a certain word meant as she was making dinner. I know it shocked her because she whirled around so fast that her oversized sweater brushed the stove and effectively set her on fire. Never cook near an open flame while wearing synthetic fabric, friends. The silver lining to this near disaster is that she was able to buy some time before answering me while my dad tried to beat out the flames and I stood in the background yelling, "Stop, drop, and roll, Mom! Stop, drop, and roll!" I am very helpful in emergency situations.

As soon as my mother had removed the charred bits of sweater and collected her composure, she sat me down and explained the meaning of what the girls had been talking about. I was completely aghast. I did not know people even did that with their body parts.

The conversation on the bus was the first of many I overheard that year. It was not what I had expected from the seventh grade. Do you know what I expected from the seventh grade? I mean, I started the year carrying a Lisa Frank backpack, if that tells you anything. (It tells you I had impeccable taste, that's what it tells you. Sure, everyone else was carrying backpacks emblazoned with No Doubt stickers, but whatever.) I went into seventh grade expecting to be inducted into some sort of exclusive club for newly minted teenage girls. For example, just off the top of my head: a club in which all of the members have to wear something purple every day and their main symbol is a unicorn. Or perhaps one in which everyone meets three times a week in the bedroom of a stylish, artsy girl where they book babysitting jobs and sometimes solve the occasional mystery.

Okay, so maybe that notion was a result of reading a copious amount of Sweet Valley Twins and The Baby-Sitter's Club books as a child, but is it my fault the leading authors of my youth led me to believe that seventh grade was The Year of the Exclusive Club? I was ready for my initiation. Plus, I was an excellent babysitter. And who doesn't want a built-in group of friends? It's literally promised right in the theme song.

Sure, I figured I'd probably be the Mallory of the group, but that was better than nothing. Mallory, my fictional doppelgänger, gave me hope. If Mallory, with her unruly hair and glasses and love of reading could make it into The Baby-Sitters Club, then I could definitely make it in seventh grade. I had read every single book in both series and all of the teen magazines I could get my hands on. I was studiously prepared for junior high. Except nowhere in either series did it talk about anything other than the occasional chaste kiss. Instead I got a completely different education as I listened to my classmates talk while I spun my locker combination. I wasn't ready for this. Everything was moving too fast and I couldn't keep up. I was stuck in the tension between wanting to be where everyone else was and not wanting to do the things I was hearing about.

This is where shame seeps in, through the tiny cracks in our confidence. I felt different, embarrassed by my naïveté, my fumbling awkwardness through coming of age. I mean, I knew about Coming Of Age. I had watched plenty of John Hughes films in my day. I was a huge fan of *The*

Breakfast Club. It's just that I thought we'd all be coming of age when we were, you know, of age. Not when we were twelve. I had just gotten my first American Girl doll two years before. I was wearing a training bra. That I didn't even need! I felt ashamed that I didn't understand it and ashamed by being excluded from it at the same time.

———✦———

As a teenager I was incredibly self-conscious of my small stature. When I was in high school, a newfangled invention hit the shelves of stores across the country: silicone bra inserts. As someone who spent a lot of time and energy devising the absolute best way to stuff her bra, these little slabs of silicone were the best things that had ever happened to me. I had tried everything. Tissues. Socks. Discarded shoulder pads from my mother's eighties-era blazers sewn together in layers. I even made a valiant attempt to duplicate the scene in *Now and Then* where the short redhead stuffs her bra using balloons filled with Jell-O pudding. I was dedicated to my cause is what I'm saying.

Eventually, I spent a week's pay on a little box with two silicone slabs inside. My sister said they looked like chicken cutlets, but I didn't care. I took to wearing them every day, lovingly washing them each night and laying them out on the bathroom sink to dry. This was highly traumatizing for my father. The unadvertised benefit of these accessories was that they inhibited any sort of access to off-limits areas.

Case in point. I was leaned back against the wall, kissing my boyfriend, when I felt his hand wander up my shirt and linger at the edge of my bra. As the full realization of what was happening hit me, I shoved him backwards with all my might. Two very distinct things were running through my mind. I was sticking staunchly to the rules of conduct to which I had pledged to abide the night I got my own True Love Waits ring. Plus, just as his fingers brushed past the satin of my Victoria's Secret, I realized if I let him cop a feel, he would wind up with a handful of molded jelly. So say what you will about stuffing your bra, but for this girl it was like a modern-day chastity belt. This is probably what Paul meant when he talked about putting on the full armor of God. (Just kidding. This is definitely not what Paul meant.)

The only problem with my beloved bra inserts, tiny thing really, was that in the hot summer weather they were unbearably uncomfortable. During my sophomore year of college, the air conditioning in my car went out, and so I did what every poor college student does in a situation like that. Absolutely nothing. I was living on ramen noodles, which meant I was driving around in the Georgia heat sweating profusely. Or as we like to call it in the South, "glistening." One day I couldn't take it anymore so, while sitting at a stoplight, I fished the silicone inserts out and threw them in my glove compartment. It was such sweet relief that I promptly forgot about them, and over the course of the summer they went and melted in that glove compartment.

Later that fall I got pulled over for the very first time. The officer said I was driving erratically and wanted to know if I'd been drinking and where I was returning from. I was not drinking, I informed him, I just wasn't a very good driver. Apparently that's not the sort of thing you're supposed to say to the campus police. Additionally, I was returning home from Bible study, and so I said I was probably just drunk on the Holy Spirit. This is the point in the traffic stop in which I learned that particular officer possessed little to no sense of humor. Which made what happened next even worse.

He leaned on my window, peered at me over his mirrored sun-glasses, and then asked for my license and registration. Which I dutifully retrieved from my glove compartment. Except I had forgotten the whole thing about how my silicone inserts had melted inside there during the summer. Turns out, in the cooler weather they had re-congealed into a large, rubbery blob with bits and pieces of paper stuck to it. Including one state registration for my 1998 Chevy Cavalier.

I tentatively held the jelly-like mass out toward the officer, and with as cheerful a voice as I could muster, said, "Um, it's kind of laminated."

He stared at me for a full minute before letting me off with a warning, which was the second time my fake silicone bra inserts saved me from my own dubious actions.

⟶

It's because I'm so familiar with such things that I sometimes mentor the college-age girls I attend church with. And by "mentor," I mean they hang out on my couch and tell me all about their problems while I listen and hope fervently that God will grant me the wisdom to know what they need. Sometimes it's affirmation, sometimes it's consolation, but often-times I see the shame etched across their faces and know exactly where the conversation is leading as they stumble to start it.

Maybe a boy slipped his hand up her shirt, too, and she didn't have the shield of stuffing between them like I did. Maybe she stripped down and loved a boy all the way past innocence. Maybe someone stole from her and called her ruined. Most of the time the details vary, but the theme is the same. "I just feel so dirty." I hear it over and over again, even if they've only gone as far as the thought of things.

It's hard to be a woman at this intersection of cultures, where the world tells us sex sells but the church tells us to be a good girl, as though our very woman-ness is bad. I've also spoken to countless women who have saved themselves only to struggle with the sudden pressure to embrace their sexuality when they reach the marriage bed. One of my friends confided, "It's like my entire life I heard that wanting sex was bad, that sexual acts were dirty, and then I got married and was expected to jump straight into doing all those 'dirty' things with enthusiasm. It was so hard for me not to feel ashamed every time we were intimate on our hon-eymoon because I was so conditioned to think of sexual things as wrong." *Preach.* This is so true of so many of our stories.

I love weddings. I've been married for a decade, and sometimes I still have to restrain myself from buying wedding magazines while I stand in the checkout line at the grocery store. If it were socially acceptable to be a wedding crasher, I would absolutely take it up as a hobby. I would just show up at random stone chapels and gush over how beautiful everything is. And eat cake.

At one wedding I recall, the church was in bloom with garlands of flowers spilling out into the aisles while handsomely tuxedoed men ushered loved ones to their white satin covered seats. It was a place befitting a beautiful celebration, a uniting of love between two souls who happened to find each other in this world of six billion options. (This alone is a sweet miracle.) Then the minister began to speak, and instead of reflecting on the sacred gravity of making a covenant, I found myself recoiling at his words.

The bride, he informed us, had not saved herself for marriage. Because of this the groom, he added, in an act of godly generosity had proven himself able to overcome such sin to take her as a wife.

I was facing the flower-draped arbor from the groom's side. He and I go way back, and I know just where his hands have wandered. But not a word was uttered about his indiscretions. Instead he got a public pat on the back, with the preacher calling him a modern-day Hosea.

I wanted to throw my arms around this bride who only moments before had walked down the aisle with her face radiant, now crimson cheeked at his chiding under the guise of the gospel at her expense. This didn't sound like grace. This sounded like a morality lesson thinly veiled as a marriage blessing. I cringed in my seat as she stood there in white taking heat instead of vows.

As they were pronounced husband and wife, I thought of the way the Bible instructs men to approach and live out their marriage: "Husbands, love your wives, just as Christ loved the church and gave himself for her to make her holy, cleansing her with the washing of water by the word. He did this to present the church to himself in splendor, without spot or wrinkle or anything like that, but holy and blameless" (Eph. 5:25–27). Everything in the wedding's sanctuary symbolized that verse. And yet a preacher used his pulpit to publicly spill shame onto a woman's white dress like a scarlet letter.

I thought of the story in John 8, when two lovers were tangled up in adultery but only one was dragged out of bed and in front of a crowd for condemnation. I imagined Jesus tracing His finger through the dirt in front of that crowd, and I wondered if we are so obsessed with a purity culture within the church that we must drive home the point from the altar. Never mind that with a slate wiped clean by grace, true love *had* waited. But I guess that sentiment doesn't sell thin gold bands emblazoned with the phrase to teenage girls.

———————

I lost my virginity the day after the man I was sure I was going to marry sat across from me in a crowded restaurant and told me he didn't see a future that held the two of us together.

The next day I ran into an old flame, and he asked if I wanted to go away for the weekend. It sounded like fun and I decided to be impulsive. "But I'm not going to sleep with you or anything," I told him. Yet I slipped lingerie under my jeans and striped sweater, because my need to be wanted outweighed my need to be cautious.

Later that night I slipped into bed beside him and decided not to say no.

It's important to me that the truth is apparent in my story: I had sex because I wanted to. No one coerced me. I just wanted to feel connected to someone. Fueled by rejection, it was a situation that had all the makings of a bad Lifetime movie.

But shame can be cruel, and then shame can be crueler. A friend of mine, sitting on a gray couch in an apartment overlooking the city, told me she was so in love with the man of her dreams that when he led her to bed, she followed willingly. He had promised to marry her. Afterwards he stood up, pulled his pants on, and said—with his still shirtless back turned—that now he knew she wasn't the woman God intended him to marry, because a godly woman would have resisted his advances. He left her there, all uncovered in the sheets, and she rose and covered herself in the shame he left behind. The next time she saw him was on the following Sunday, her in a pew, and him in the pulpit as he offered the morning prayer in his role as elder. It's been a decade since she told me about that day, and I still want to weep every time I think about it, because sometimes shame comes from only one moment of confusion in your story.

"It is not dirty to desire," I tell the girl on my couch, and she looks dubious but hopeful. "Women were created to be sensual. This was our making, when Eve was all curves and passion. It is inherently feminine, what drew her and Adam together in the Garden. It's not shameful to feel. You are not used or damaged goods, or any less valuable than you were before. You are worth more than rubies to a God who loves extravagantly, and the status of your virginity does not change that. You are worth exactly the same to me and to anyone else who is worthy of your love."

I also tell her, most certainly, about the Song of Solomon, the part that repeats three times to "not stir up or awaken love until the appropriate time" (Song 8:4), because intimacy leads to tangled emotions. This sort of vulnerability, I tell her, is the sacred kind, designed to be entrusted to the care of the one you're in covenant with. Awakened love is meant to be fulfilled at the marriage altar. But I do not tell her she is dirty. And I do not tell her she is bad.

There are two separate narratives the purity movement teaches subtly about sex: A) guys want it all the time and just can't help themselves, and B) girls should not even want it at all until they're married, at which time they should meet all their husband's sexual needs without ever having acknowledged their own. We're taught to be willing wives without a foundation for embracing the sensuality that the lover in Song of Solomon esteems of his bride.

But this way of thinking completely suppresses a woman's sexuality and denies her the opportunity to understand her sexual urges. It creates a perfect pathway for shame to seep in and twist a young girl's thinking. If wanting it is bad and she wants it, she may as well swim in the depths of that pool because she's already bad. It is a missive full of shame. As Heather Davis Nelson writes, "Shame's message is, 'I am bad,' and needs an identity shift and relational connection. Shames feels like it's welded onto you."[1]

We owe more to our girls. We owe them better than creating an environment surrounding sensuality that welds shame to them.

Once my much older male boss pressed himself up against the back of me as I bent over a filing cabinet, and I only shifted uncomfortably away. Shame had been so wholly welded on to me that I thought maybe it was my fault, that I had invited it with my over-friendliness or the snug fit of my pants. I want our girls to find their freedom first so they never have to wonder if they inadvertently welcomed sexual harassment.

One curriculum in particular taught us that we should confess all of our sexual exploits to a man before we even began a dating relationship because men had the right to a virgin bride and should be able to refuse a woman before becoming enmeshed with their, as they called it, baggage.

It's a little awkward to share that on a first date.

It's devastating when he walks away.

—

When we were teenagers, gas cost less than a dollar and a raven-haired boy named Jeff would take the T-tops off his Trans-Am as we drove winding roads through the Georgia mountains for hours. I told him about that night I couldn't take back.

"You know it doesn't change how I see you, right?" he said tenderly. "It doesn't change how God sees you either."

It was the personification of grace to me because he shared in my sadness, spoke love to me, and refused to cast shame. There was no romance between us then, just a deep friendship and a trust in the conviction of his words that set me on the path to freedom. We did not yet know that Jeff was meant to be my husband.

Years later we waited together for a wedding night, and he never once held grace over me like a victory flag. We shut the door to the honeymoon suite, swathed in white roses, and I felt wanted and holy and blameless.

I was unashamed.

CHAPTER 7

Piece of Glass

Mirror, mirror, here I stand. Who is the fairest in the land?
—The Brothers Grimm, *Snow White*

"What about Kayla?" one of the boys asked.

Our English teacher had stepped out, and during this unplanned intermission from learning, our classroom turned into a real-life version of Hot or Not. I chewed nervously on my hair as I waited for my rating. I didn't want one, but in junior high you're conscripted into such games. Participation is not what you would call voluntary.

The boy doling out the verdicts was a friend, so I thought I might be safe from public mortification. "Kayla? No. She's a total dog," came the reply, and I made it all the way to the hallway before I let the tears fall behind the door of my locker.

That was the day I knew for sure that I was ugly.

I'd had an inkling of it before, the one time a family friend mentioned what a shame it was that I ended up with my father's nose, or the time someone close to me said offhandedly while glancing at my school picture, "Well, it's a good thing you're smart because this sure isn't pretty." Granted, I looked like the cameraman had caught me mid-sneeze but still, what I heard was, "You're a hideous troll."

I had, on several occasions, examined myself fairly closely in my black wicker bedroom mirror. I didn't like my ears (too elf-like) or my nose (too dad-like) or my gangly, skinny arms. My hair was frizzy and my skin was so pale that it would rival the main character of a vampire novel, without even the added benefit of sparkling. But I had a nice smile and pretty eyes (if a little buggy), and I figured I sat solidly in the average area of a six. So sure, I knew I wasn't a knockout, but assumed I was okay looking. Cute, maybe. Until the day I saw myself through the eyes of a boy who called me a dog, and from then on, all I saw in the mirror was ugly.

I didn't see the beauty in eyes that dance when I laugh or a smile that genuinely lights up my face for the people I love. I didn't see pretty in a thick mass of wavy hair that one day my newborn son would curl around his fist as he gazed up at me. The only thing that registered regarding my appearance was that I was, as he said, "a total dog." I traded my view for his four-word phrase, and the mirror became my mortal enemy. There was nothing I hated more in the world than my own reflection.

(Except maybe collard greens. Collard greens are awful and no one should be forced to eat them, even if your sweet great-grandma Sybil did grow them in her garden and cook them up just for you because you pretended to like them once out of politeness.)

This is probably where you flip over the book to check out my picture on the back cover to see if I am actually the troll-like creature I've been describing. I will not judge you for this. During the time I suffered the worst from my low self-esteem, I would flip over the book jacket on every book in the bookstore to see what the author looked like. If I thought she was attractive, I shelved it because I figured she must not really know the first thing about struggling with self-esteem, on account of how she looked like she could do shampoo commercials. It's the sort of irony that belongs in an Alanis Morissette song.

I actually really love that back cover photo, partially because I made friends with people who are makeup artists and professional photographers, and this has served me quite well in my adult life. I took that whole "pick your friends wisely" advice to heart. Plus, I suffer from Chandler Bing Syndrome, whereby I cannot take a photo without making an incredibly awkward face. The fact that my parents paid for any of my school pictures is a testament to their love for me. They did not *display* many of them, but they bought them, and that counts for something.

To combat this, and to keep my very first Official Author Photo from looking as though I'd just tasted something awful, my best friend danced around goofily while the photographer snapped pictures of me laughing. This is the epitome of squad goals, if you ask me. I was going for Cheerful Looking Girl That You Would Want to Strike Up a Conversation With at Your Local Coffee Shop, and after about 236 shots, we ended up somewhere around Girl Who Seems Slightly Afraid to Stop Smiling, but all in all I'd say it was a good team effort.

So I feel very endeared toward this particular photo because I was happy that day, surrounded by friends who were cheering me on in the pursuit of my dreams of writing a book. But also because I no longer loathe the sight of myself on film.

My fifteen-year-old self never saw that day coming.

———————

Recently my friend Amy joked that her entire life would have turned out differently if she had only owned a decent straightening iron in junior high, and I was all, "You have just defined everything I know to be true." My hair was so wild that one day the school bully who sat behind me in English class emptied an entire stapler into my hair and I didn't even notice until I went to wash my hair that night, whereupon I discovered a million tiny staples stuck in my curls.

The Bible talks about a woman's hair being her crowning glory, but mine seemed somehow defective, all wild and unruly and completely indecisive. The sides wind in tight spirals, while the back falls in loose waves and the front just frizzes, stick straight. I've broken more than one brush in an attempt to pull the bristles through my thick tangles. It is absolutely untamable, as evidenced by the fact that any effort to contain it can turn the simplest hair accessory into a deadly weapon. Once I bowed my head in church, and a bobby pin shot out of my hair and bounced off the neck of the cute boy sitting in the pew in front of me. This is probably the real reason the Bible instructed women to cover their heads while praying.

It doesn't matter how I attempt to style my hair, I just always end up looking like a failed beauty pageant contestant. It's big. This is why I prescribe to the age-old adage, "The higher the hair, the closer to God." Not because I want to, necessarily, but because if you can't beat 'em, join 'em. My hair is currently growing out into the exact shape of an isosceles triangle. (That sentence is the only time I've ever needed to use geometry, despite what my tenth-grade math teacher said.)

One morning before school, Scarlette stood in front of her mirror and sobbed because she didn't like her hair. I understand this sort of crisis, so I took down her ponytail and told her I would do her hair however she liked, but I needed her to tell me what she wanted. She cried, "I don't know! I just need it to be BEAUTIFUL and COMPLICATED! I just wish you knew what was best for me, Mommy!" I was left standing there bewildered, thinking, *Well, it's definitely complicated . . .*

It's complicated because women are besieged with imaging that suggests our life's success hinges on pretty. It's complicated because the unspoken expectation is for us to be smooth and flawless and attractive. It's complicated because our acceptance has been based on appearances and has led us to believe our worth is all tangled up with our physique.

After I gave birth to my second baby, my bum started a slow descent down my thighs, and so I decided to be like Fergie and start working on my fitness. I do feel a certain responsibility to take care of the body I've been given, especially because my polycystic ovary syndrome means I often feel like my body is working against me. I wanted to feel strong and fit, but I also felt a little bit of pressure to get my pre-baby shape back. I worried about how my tummy had come all untucked during the time I spent nurturing the baby in my womb. I felt annoyed that the phrase "post-baby body" is even a thing, as though society wants to quickly erase all evidence of the miracle to which women are a testament when they grow an ENTIRE HUMAN BEING in their body for nine months.

Keeping up appearances is such a heavy burden placed on women. Do you know what my husband does before he goes to bed? He slathers some essential oil on his head where he's got a bit of a bald spot, and then he calls it a day. Sometimes he does a few push-ups or hits the boxing bag, which I encourage less for health reasons and more because I enjoy the view when he is shirtless. At thirty-three his inky black hair is struck through with shocks of white, and he doesn't feel even a twinge of pressure to dye it. He just gets to embrace looking distinguished. Meanwhile, approximately eighty-six different boxes of hair dye for women line the beauty aisle, all promising to "hide the grays." And the reason he doesn't have a collection of anti-wrinkle night creams cluttering up his side of the sink is not because he isn't aging but because men aren't inundated with advertisements suggesting that holding onto their youthful appearance is paramount to their value.

My college dorm room was decorated in cheerful shades of teal and yellow, a marriage of the colors my best friend and I both favored. Piles of rumpled clothing littered the floor, and snapshots from disposable cameras papered the walls. A handful of brightly colored sticky notes framed the full-length mirror on the back of our door, each one offering encouragement in my roommate's signature loopy cursive. "You are fearfully and wonderfully made." "You are beautiful." "You are worth more than rubies," they read, exhorting me with biblical prose in an effort to teach me how to love myself. I stood in front of that mirror every day and brushed black mascara over my lashes while surrounded by those words, and I tried to believe them. I wanted to believe them. But by that point my self-esteem was a veritable wasteland. I couldn't bring myself to get out of bed some days, let alone face the world when my face was the very thing I wanted to keep hidden. I draped my hair in front of it, letting it fall over my eyes, keeping me veiled, both literally and figuratively, behind it.

The quote affixed to my mirror these days is from the heart of my friend Kaitlyn, who wrote, "We have got beauty all wrong, all upside down and inside out. And that's the problem. Beauty is inside out and we're looking outside in."[1] I think about this statement as I swipe sheer candy-pink gloss over my lips, how "people look at the outward appearance, but the LORD looks at the heart" (1 Sam. 16:7 NIV).

I'm only wearing the barest hint of makeup today. My newborn son is sleeping tied up in a swath of fabric across my chest. No amount of concealer can cover the circles under my eyes, and I feel (in Scarlette's words) beautiful and complicated. I find it's a hard thing to embrace the promise that inner beauty is deeply valued, while living in a culture that constantly extolls the virtues of outer beauty, expecting perfection.

———

"Your eyebrows look so great," I told Bre as we sat curled on the worn leather sofa in our favorite coffee shop.

She looked up in surprise. "Do you know you're the second person to tell me that recently? And do you know for my whole life I've hated my eyebrows? They're one of the things I'm most insecure about."

I personally am hopeless when it comes to my eyebrows. I can never seem to get them to match. The one time I tried plucking them, I may have slightly overdone it and ended up walking around looking like I was perpetually surprised for weeks. I realize I could get them waxed, but I cannot get onboard with a scenario that involves paying money for someone to spread hot wax on my face and then rip it off. That seems like a terrible idea. But Bre's eyebrows were all perfectly aligned and shaped, so I mentioned it to her.

"I guess now that thick eyebrows are in, I'm just naturally in style," she remarked.

"Do you know what I dislike about myself?" I mused. "My elbows. For my whole life I've hated how bony my elbows are. I'm always self-consciously covering them. And it's not like elbows are a thing that all of a sudden are going to be 'in.' No one's ever going to be like, 'Oh, great elbows.'"

On the other hand, no one has ever seemed outwardly disgusted by my elbows either. This is probably because no one even pays attention to other people's elbows. Except me. Because I dislike mine, I always notice the elbows of people I meet and then think to myself, *Self, why can't I have nice elbows like her?* And then I get a little jealous that they can just prop their elbows up on the table like it's no big thing. Sure, I can claim I'm not putting my elbows up on tables because of manners, but the truth is, it's because I don't want anyone to see them.

(I should not even be telling you this. I once heard Shania Twain say that you should never tell anyone what you perceive to be your own flaws because then they'll look for them. Now everyone is going to be sneaking peeks at my elbows.)

This might not be so disturbing if it weren't for the fact that I dislike so many other things about my body. It's not as though I feel pretty good about everything else but side-eye my elbows. It's like, I dislike everything, *including* my elbows. This is not good for the soul. Or for my love of tank tops in the summer time. The need to wear a three-quarter-length sleeve against the need to not be burning up in the Georgia heat has me living in the tension.

As women, we are assaulted daily by messages of expectation about who we should be. The imagery presented to us as a standard of perfection is polished and Photoshopped and rarely reflective of real-life bodies. My elbows are just a symbol of how I feel about my own body overall, the way it's all sharp angles and lacking the curves I see on the magazine covers in checkout lines. Television tells us we should be tall and lithe and have perfectly white teeth, like we're not all addicted to Starbucks. Magazines tell us we should be able to "Lose the weight in ten days" or to "Get glowing summer skin." I cannot turn on a radio station without someone telling me I should get some part of my body nipped or tucked or lasered off. I'm not even against women making choices for themselves to do those things, but I resent how my drive to the store is saturated by the message that I *should* do them, when I just want to listen to the latest hits.

Even the subliminal messages are strong. In commercials a man drags a razor across his face, cutting a clean path through a thick beard on a strong jaw. Women, however, appear to be shaving shapely legs that are already hairless. Seriously, look closely at an advertisement for women's razors. *Of course* the razor glides easily through the thick foam of shaving cream when there is no hair on their legs to begin with. This is completely unrealistic. After a cold winter I need about three razors per leg. These subtle messages keep us conditioned to a standard of beauty that expects an unreasonable amount of perfectionism in women. The pressure to look irresistible is so impossible that it leaves us feeling invisible. Or wishing we were.

Learning to love the way that I was fearfully and wonderfully made was hard work. It didn't come from a man who loved me or a best friend who encouraged me or even the very beneficial purchase of a straightening iron. Mostly it came time-traveling into my present day from Romans 12, with Paul saying, "I appeal to you . . . to present your bodies as a living sacrifice, holy and acceptable to God, which is your spiritual worship. Do not be conformed to this world, but be transformed by the renewal of your mind" (vv. 1–2 ESV). It's probably the closest I've ever come to being athletic as an adult, the way I've conditioned myself to replace all my negative self-talk with truthful affirmations. It came slowly, through training and discipline, more marathon than sprint. (I think. I've never run an actual race, so make of that metaphor what you will.)

But after the hard work comes the reward.

I kept up the tradition my best friend started in that third-floor dorm room, and I memorized Bible verses that said things such as, "You are absolutely beautiful, my darling; there is no imperfection in you" (Song 4:7).

I plastered them on my mirror and in my wallet and on my dashboard. I repeated them to myself as I ventured to the store with no makeup on and allowed myself to feel utterly exposed. I took up yoga, primarily because instead of running, they let you lie down on the floor in the fetal position and call it exercise, and as I stretch one arm over the other I think about Ephesians 2:10 and how we are God's handiwork.

"Don't you yourselves know that you are God's temple and that the Spirit of God lives in you?" (1 Cor. 3:16). I meditate on these words as I fold my body in on itself, arched across the pale blue mat. They call this position "downward dog," but I don't call myself that anymore.

I have a new standard of beauty.

Abandoned

You can't stay in your corner of the Forest waiting for others
to come to you. You have to go to them sometimes.
—A. A. Milne

Last night I ended up sleeping in the baby's room, so when Scarlette went to climb in my bed the next morning, I wasn't there. Since she is not at all prone to the dramatic, this led to her sitting in the hallway clutching her stuffed giraffe and lamenting, "I just don't know where Mommy is! Who is going to take care of me? Who is going to take care of Ridley? I can't take care of a baby all by myself! I'm just a little kid! I'M JUST A LITTLE KID! I can't use the stove!"

My heart felt all tender toward her plight, so I called out to her, hoping to soothe her fears. She peeked her head in the doorway and said cheerfully, "Oh! You still live here! Can you make me some pancakes?" Clearly I am an important cog in this family unit.

She was afraid I had left her, which is understandable because isn't that what we all secretly fear? That we are Teflon and that our people won't stick? We worry that one single rejection is going to be the sum total of our relationships going forward. We are secretly afraid, deep down, that once someone really gets to know us, they aren't going to be all in for our mess, and then they're going to leave us. We think this is inevitable, the leaving, that it's only a matter of time before we're left alone again. (Or maybe it's just me, in which case you are now privy to all my deepest secrets.)

I think this is one of the biggest draws of social media, because it gives us an instant, external validation that we are still wanted. It reassures us that we are liked, literally. One of my friends has a teenage daughter who deletes any picture she posts on Instagram that doesn't get as many likes as she wants. She says it's embarrassing to have too few likes on a photo because the amount of likes tells other people whether or not you're a cool person.

I don't need Instagram to tell me that. I have a five-year-old. This morning I pulled on my typical super stylish preschool car line attire: yoga pants and a tank top. Scarlette walked in, looked at me, shook her head and said, "Mommy. You can't just keep wearing your jammies ALL DAY all da time! You needa wear CLOTHES sometimes. You know! REAL clothes! Just try it!" I think it's apparent that I am the epitome of cool.

I really want to have it all together, but there are a few things standing in my way. One is my penchant for repeatedly hitting the snooze button until I barely have time to brush my teeth in the mornings. The other is that I have two children. But that's not the reason I'm standoffish at school pickup in the afternoons. The truth is that I'm afraid of living uncovered. I don't want to talk to you in the school car line if I don't have concealer on because I feel overly exposed, and then my fear spills out in stilted interactions as my body looks for a place to hide. I am always on the brink and ready to flee, poised to run. Because if I leave first, I don't have to risk the aftermath of being abandoned.

Alone.

This is what our insecurity steals from us, the freedom to live breathless with wonder rather than out of breath from running away. Shame creates a flight pattern in us that sends us into hiding. It sends us deep into the garden, frantically fashioning garments out of leaves. It erodes our trust and makes us suspicious of other people's motives. When we embrace shame, we consequently turn our backs on the outstretched arms of the people who are offering us the very acceptance we crave. When we accumulate our past rejections, we create a story for ourselves that says no one will want us. We clothe ourselves in restless insecurity and let it mask us for fear of facing the world without a filter. Insecurity conceals the very things that God meant to reveal.

This is not the story that was written for us. We were born into an inheritance of belonging. As Curt Thompson says, "Shame turns us away from others, but we see God responding to our shame by drawing us into community."[1] It is only shame that causes us to hide ourselves for fear of rejection.

The day I met my husband was the same day he was baptized. This is the sort of thing that happens when you grow up in the Bible Belt. A friend of a friend invites you to go to his brother's baptism, despite the fact you've never met his brother. It was right before our senior year of high school, and I sat in the balcony of the church while a man in white robes dipped Jeff down into the baptistery.

Afterwards we all went back to his house for finger foods. I nibbled on a canapé, noticed his eyes, and I was done for. He became one of my closest friends, and over the next few years I was at his house almost more than my own. We went for long drives, I nursed a secret crush, and he continued to date girls who looked like Kardashians.

I fell asleep on his couch the November that I spent my first Thanksgiving alone. It was my freshman year of college, and I felt a bit lost in the aftermath of my parents' divorce. My family was fractured and I was faltering a little as I tried to figure out where I fit into life that was restructuring itself around me. He printed out the lyrics to Jimmy Eat World's "The Middle" on a sheet of pale yellow paper, which I kept folded up and slowly fading in my wallet for years. I pulled it out to read it often, a sweet, rhyming reminder that everything was going to be all right.

I think this is why I fell in love with Jeff, because he saw me when I was still trying to hide.

We got married three days before Christmas, standing in front of an evergreen tree that was meant to be symbolic. He wore a pinstriped tuxedo, standing with his hands clasped in front of him. I pinned fresh flowers in my hair and made my way to him bathed in lace and candlelight. We stood at that altar in black and white, and we gave everything to that "I do." We wrote our own vows, and he said, "Nothing you have done, or are yet to do, will separate my heart from yours." There were no shades of gray.

So when it broke, it crashed down hard, slipped right through our fingers, and shattered as we stood next to an incubator and watched our newborn daughter struggle for breath. Our entrance to new parenthood was tangled up in tiny IV lines and monitors that measured missing heartbeats. Life moved as though almost outside of time, slow and tense and separate. Altogether we counted 156 days inside those walls, and it could have been years for how the gravity of it felt.[2]

On a Tuesday in February, the air in the NICU was thick like a humid Georgia day, saturated with the heaviness of wearing nothing but heartache and hope. One minute my daughter was breathing, and the next minute she wasn't. One minute I was bouncing cheerfully out of an elevator, and the next I was banished to a waiting room while doctors and nurses worked frantically to resuscitate her.

What I don't tell people about the day that she flatlined is where Jeff and I were. They just assume we were together, fingers interlaced like that day at the altar. They don't know about the distance. As we waited to find out whether or not our daughter was still alive, I sat stiffly in a small blue chair just outside of the NICU. My husband, overwhelmed with anguish, got in our car and drove north, through the night and through his pain, up a long stretch of highway in the opposite direction of the hospital. He disappeared behind taillights, and I didn't see his tears through my own.

I always thought the rending of garments seemed a bit overdramatic until that very moment, when I sat alone in a hospital room with my husband gone and my daughter dying. Sometimes when emotional pain is too much to bear, your body just shuts down, whether from shock or self-preservation. I sat with my arms wound around my waist to hold myself together, stricken with the thought that I had just lost everything.

I felt, in the deepest sense, that he had abandoned me.

(I also felt that way literally on account of how he was my ride home.)

Where we had knit our hearts together, I felt it wrench apart. I did not think it could ever recover. These were all my fears crashing in on one another and burying me beneath them. It felt like my last rites, all ashes to ashes and dust to dust as I sat rooted to the spot and watched the life flicker out of everything I loved. It was a desolate broken.

When I was standing on the edge of losing everything, I was held up only by the remnants of my faith, the very hem of a garment. I wrote in *Anchored*, "As I stood there at the glass, I knew that if I walked back into that room only to find myself holding her lifeless form against my still beating heart, everything else would change and God would not. That in the middle of this crushing chaos, spinning senseless with heartache, this would be constant and I would cling to it and it would not fail me. That if all else were lost, I would have this hope as an anchor."[3] It seemed as if it was the only thing left.

An hour away my husband sat in the shower sobbing as the water ran cold. I matched it in the intensity of my emotions toward him. The danger of anger isn't always when it burns hot and rages outward. Sometimes it runs ice cold, sealing off love behind an impenetrable frozen fortress. I did not move toward him to soothe his pain, and so I didn't know the depth of his fear. I only knew I was left behind.

As the time passed the hurt only grew. I couldn't mend it because my hands were full of baby and my heart was full of splintered sadness. Neither of us knew where to start. It sat in shattered pieces until we tried to put it back together, and then it didn't fit like before. Nothing was easy and light and carefree.

I thought about the way my parents' marriage broke to pieces. Rarely does something break without collateral damage, tiny shards to pick through with bloodied fingers. I clutched at the fragments, unsure if I wanted to trace the edges with glue and place them back permanently because I was afraid of risking again. We were both afraid of risking.

In the framed engagement photo gracing our mantel, we lean against a bright red wall and gaze at each other with an affection that feels both familiar and foreign. I never expected the portrait of us to shift from vibrant color to muddled shades of gray. I never expected that love wouldn't feel black and white anymore or that our gazes would shift, that we would stare across a room hollow-eyed as we toiled through the hardest parts. I never thought I'd wear a wedding ring and feel lonely. Sitting in a sermon listening to a pastor preach about how if we really had faith in God we should never feel alone in any circumstance, I brushed away tears with the back of my hand. *What is wrong with me?* I wondered. Because all I had was faith. If that was enough, then why was I still so lonely?

Our marriage stayed stagnant for a few years, until we talked about separating and I packed up the car. I laid in the antique bed in Laura Anne's guest room and cried because I didn't know what home looked like anymore. She and I watched out her bay window as Scarlette ran gleefully around her backyard, collecting pinecones and chasing Laura's new puppy. "What are you going to do?" Laura asked me as we sat shoulder to shoulder. I leaned my head on her arm.

I drove home.

———⚓

While I was pregnant this past winter, one of Scarlette's friends at school was diagnosed with leukemia. It was supposed to be the best kind of cancer to have, if you had to have cancer. The prognosis was good, and we sent cards and gifts to him in the hospital. The school took up a collection for his family, and I tucked our contribution inside Scarlette's handmade card.

"Why did you put some monies in Nathan's card?" she asked me. I explained to her it's very expensive to be in the hospital, and that when she was sick in the hospital, people did the same thing for us. "It's just one way we can help," I told her.

"Oh! Well, then, let's give him some MORE monies!" she exclaimed.

"Sorry, baby, that's all the money Mommy has," I told her. Since I rarely keep cash on hand, I'd plucked the crisp bills out of a Christmas card someone had sent us.

Later that day she went to chapel, where she stood up during the time for prayer requests and asked everyone to pray for me because I was going to have a baby, and babies had to be in the hospital, and hospitals were VERY expensive.

"And," she exclaimed from her little spot in front of the stained glass windows, "we don't have any monies for the hospital because Mommy gave all our monies to Nathan!"

I keep faithfully trying to impress meaningful life lessons on her, and she keeps completely misconstruing them.

Like how I spend a lot of time reading *The Jesus Storybook Bible* to her and elaborating on the meaning behind the stories. I know this is making an impression on her because when it was Cow Appreciation Day at Chick-Fil-A, I told her we were going to dress up like cows so we could visit the restaurant and get a free lunch. Scarlette ran out of the room and returned with all of her musical instruments gathered in her arms. "Okay! I am ready to be in the parade!" she told me.

"No, honey, there's no parade," I said, slightly confused.

She answered impatiently, "Yes I KNOW dat, Mommy. I am going to BE da cow parade. I'm going to march in my cow costume around and around and play all of my instruments until the walls fall down!"

And that is the story of how my four-year-old confused Cow Appreciation Day with the Bible, like she was Joshua, and our local fast-food haunt was a modern-day Jericho. I'm not sure where I went off course in teaching her this story, but I want to raise her right so, like Paul, I continue on steadfastly in prayer.

The same day that she declared our bankruptcy to her classmates, I was admitted to the hospital for pregnancy complications. Later that week, her friend Nathan took a turn for the worse and then tragically passed away. Her father and I tried our best to explain death to her, lying close on her pink-and-white striped sheets as she tried to work out the thin veil between earth and heaven. She struggled over the finiteness of it all—how someone can be here one day, and then suddenly they're not. "Why can't God just send people back?" she wanted to know. I stroked her hair and talked about the celestial mystery of how all things are made new.

A few days later I was admitted to the hospital again and this was the day she became afraid of losing me. "Nathan was in the hospital, and then he never came back," she wept. She was afraid I would leave her, too, which ignited a period where she couldn't fall asleep on her own. Nearly every night she would work herself into a fit of tears and then be unable to quiet herself down.

"I can't calm down," she would choke out through strangled sobs. I would lie down next to her as she snuggled in close, chest heaving with tears that trickled down my neck. She would cling to me desperately, breath hitching as I smoothed back her hair, clutching at me as though letting go meant I might leave her alone in her grief.

"You can calm down," I said. "I can help you. We're going to take three deep breaths, okay? Ready? Let's count them: *one*, deep breath, *two*, deep breath, *three*, deep breath," slowly and steadily.

This scene is an echo.

Its first whisper took place in a wide-open hospital bay when I was sitting next to the plastic incubator that housed my baby. She couldn't find a rhythm for her breath, and I was holding mine as I watched her skin turn a mottled gray, over and over and over. Usually a nurse will lay the baby across the mother's chest, but Scarlette was so critically ill that I was not allowed to hold her. I pulled my chair up close to the porthole on the side of the incubator and turned my head sideways to lay my face next to hers. I cupped one of my hands around the whole of her body, enveloping her in my palm. And then I began to breathe, concentrating slowly on the in and out, the rise and the fall of my chest. I sang softly to her, a song about breathing, about how grace is all-surrounding like air. I sat nearly motionless for the better part of two hours until the rhythm of her breaths matched itself to mine and the alarms went silent. I did it because I was afraid she was leaving me.

All this imagery plays through my mind as I lay beside her again nearly five years later, seeking to cover her in my love, reminding her how to breathe. Eventually she quiets, then stills, this sweet, sleeping beauty on my shoulder. I linger just a little bit longer, holding her as she sleeps, because her deepest need in this moment is the comfort of my presence. I am here, and that is her reassurance.[4]

The gift of our presence is the most eternally significant gift we can offer one another. We don't need the right words; we just need to show up for one another. Simply by virtue of not disappearing, we're saying "I am present for you. I will not leave you."

———✦———

I was in the other room when I heard the baby start to fuss. I glanced at the monitor to see Scarlette walk over towards the bassinet. I wasn't sure how this was going to play out, given that she runs hot and cold on the idea of having a baby brother. Just the other morning when he was crying, she put her hands over her ears and exclaimed, "Just put him on the back porch, Mommy, I can't take it anymore!" (Then I had to explain to her that baby brothers are not the same thing as our dog Lucy.)

So I wasn't expecting the best as I watched the monitor. But instead of getting frustrated, she began stroking his head softly and said to him, "Don't worry, brother, don't worry. You don't have to be sad. Our Mommy ALWAYS comes back."

Then I had a good cry into my coffee, and not just because I was relegated to drinking decaf while nursing.

This is what I always want my children to know, that I will never walk away. If I were to write them a love letter, it would look suspiciously like the Bible, verse after verse of assurance: "I will never leave you nor forsake you" (Heb. 13:5 ESV); "I am with you always, to the end of the age" (Matt. 28:20); "because of his great love" for us (Eph. 2:4), we will never be left all alone. The reason I use Scripture as my affirmation is because it is true and it is unfailing. You can press into those promises because they are permanent. Read Romans 4:8 and repeat it until it becomes indelible on your heart: "Blessed is the person the Lord will never charge with sin." You are not abandoned. You are never alone. You are loved to the end of the age.

This is what I want my children to know about love. It is worth risking. We abandoned one another, their father and I, and then we chose each another again. He wrote in his vows that nothing would separate us. I wrote in mine that "God risked Himself on me; I will risk myself on you. And together, we will learn to love."[5]

We are taking the risk.

And we are, each of us, worth taking a risk on.

CHAPTER 9

I Love the Nineties

You had me at "hello."
—Dorothy Boyd, *Jerry Maguire*

My dad drove me to school in a little red pickup truck with
bench seats. Sometimes it was my job to rotate the stick shift through
the gears, and sometimes it was my job to make sure no feral cats had
curled up in the wheel wells overnight. But it was never my job to turn
the radio dial. It was always set on the seventies station to the sounds of
Led Zeppelin and Pink Floyd. I particularly enjoyed the humor in singing
"We don't need no education" on the way to school most mornings. (I am
easily entertained.)

This always annoyed me as a kid because I wanted to listen to my
music. I thought my dad's music was old and out of touch. I could not
understand why he wanted to listen to the Eagles over Mariah Carey. As
an adult, however, I understand the firm pull of nostalgia and why my dad
always reached for the music of his youth. I now find myself constantly
dismissing the current songs on the radio in favor of my favorites from the
era of my own adolescence.

That's right. I love the nineties.

I keep trying to instill my love of the nineties in Scarlette, much the
same way my dad tried really hard to get me to appreciate Tom Petty. One
fall evening I discovered that *Milo and Otis* was free to rent on Amazon
Prime. Filled with nostalgic memories of my love of this movie as a child,

I decided it would make for the perfect mommy/daughter movie night. When we were about twenty minutes in, all curled up on my bed with hot apple cider and watching Otis bravely follow Milo down the river, I asked tearfully, "So, Scarlette, don't you just love this movie?" She snuggled in close to my side and replied, "Actually, no, Mommy. It's kind of freaking me out over here." (I am happy to report that she responded much more positively to *Space Jam*.)

In the middle of that decade, my parents insisted I go to youth group, mostly because they thought it would be a good way for me to make new friends before high school. I needed a fresh start and this was it—a converted barn behind the Baptist church where the boys played basketball before we all gathered on oversized couches on Wednesday nights. If it had been a relationship status on Facebook, the years I spent at youth group would be marked "it's complicated." Youth group both saved me and shamed me.

I blame it on the nineties, really. It was an era of countercultural movement within the church, when we wore our What Would Jesus Do bracelets with our Scandinavian sweaters and Timberland boots. It was all very dramatic. During my junior year of high school, my youth group participated in an event called Heaven's Gates, Hell's Flames, where visitors walked through a church version of a haunted house, past a fake bus crash, and finally through a mock version of heaven and hell. Our job was to sit in the bus and then scream in faux agony during the crash portion. It felt like we were changing the world.

We formed accountability groups, for instance, to protect one another from things we deemed unsafe, like secular music. Once a boy I liked spotted a Christina Aguilera CD in my car, so he rolled down the window and threw it onto the side of the road, a spinning silver disc flying toward the brush at seventy-five miles an hour. (I think the actual unsafe thing here is throwing things out of a moving vehicle.)

We drove icy roads to Gatlinburg, Tennessee, where we spent a week at Winter Camp, listening to speakers tell us we needed to be on fire for

God. The Newsboys played watered-down rock music under strobe lights. We weren't allowed to dance, so we stood up close to the stage and just jumped up and down for hours.

We all "Kissed Dating Goodbye," vowing to pursue courtship instead, especially me because it sounded much better to tell people that Jesus was my boyfriend than to admit no one had asked me to the prom. We twisted a purity ring around a finger in a pledge, and it felt like a revolution. We went to church camp, and we camped out at church. We were insular and we were passionate. We were all going to do big things for God.

Then we became adults.

I think the reason my generation feels so restless about church is because, for many of us, that brightly painted room where the youth group met was our first sense of belonging, before we grew up and life scattered us apart. We want church to give us that connection again, but the dynamic has shifted with the passing years.

It was on a youth group sponsored trip to the skating rink that I first met Laura Anne. My parents practically forced me onto the church bus that morning, because for some reason they thought it would be a good idea for me to meet a whole bunch of new people for the first time while wearing roller skates. Never mind that I trip over my own two feet about fifteen times a day. Just yesterday my daughter was standing in the middle of the room when she suddenly fell over for no good reason. "Well, it looks like she got the clumsiness gene from you," my husband quipped. He is hilarious, that one.

I slunk down in my seat on the church bus, hoping the invisibility I had learned in junior high would serve me well and save me from potential harassment. The girl next to me struck up a conversation, a redhead who'd just moved to town from Florida. Her parents had also forced *her* on the trip to make friends, and we bonded while commiserating about our bad fortune.

Turns out our parents had the right idea because church kids are trained to be welcoming. By the time we left the skating rink, we hadn't gotten any better at staying upright on wheels, but we had acquired several new friends: a few upperclassmen, a couple of guys on the football team, a sassy blonde, and a curly-headed cheerleader. I was basically ready to star in my own version of *Saved by the (Church) Bell*. Freshman year was looming, and it looked a lot less scary from a church pew. I finally felt like I might have found a place to fit.

Church was something I knew. It was familiar in the way certain things fade into the background of everyday life, like how my grandparents' house always smelled like Corn Flakes and Pine-Sol. I had been attending church with my grandparents ever since I could remember, in starched collared dresses every Sunday morning and pleated skirts with patent leather shoes every Sunday and Wednesday night. I was accustomed to mealtimes at long tables in a fellowship hall, and I'd memorized even the most obscure books of the Bible at Vacation Bible School. But youth group was different. Youth group was bright lights and Bibles emblazoned with neon green paint. Youth group was the opposite of being seen and not heard. Youth group was forward motion. I was swept up in the momentum.

There were three rows of high-backed wooden pews in our church, just to the right of the pulpit, and this was where the youth group sat, all lined up shoulder to shoulder on Sundays. If I arrived late, slipping through the double doors during the first hymn, everyone scooted over a bit so that I could squeeze in. It was the first time anyone made room for me. I was intoxicated by it. I belonged there, I thought, in that converted barn where people lived by the Bible. I could live by those rules. I liked the way they gave me perimeters, and I stayed steadily within them, assuming the parts that chafed were there because I was in need of changing.

I don't know if you know this, but I'm a little bit sarcastic. I used to worry obsessively over this because I'm not sweet. I mean, I'm a fairly kind person, but I'm not a sweet person. This facet of my personality is in stark contrast to the rest of my identity as a southern girl. And for a long time, I felt this was in contrast to who I was as a woman of God.

The church I attended in my youth put a lot of emphasis on what it meant to be a godly woman, and the definition felt incredibly narrow. What had once felt like belonging became oppressive and restraining. Rather than encouraging me to grow gracefully in the unique personality I was created with, it now seemed to whisper to me that I wasn't Godly Woman material because I didn't fit the mold. I wasn't good enough. It was the same refrain that chorused in other areas of my life as well, but I didn't expect it to echo here in the one place that should have felt most like refuge. The fact that I heard it in my sanctuary caused such confusion in my young heart.

Oftentimes when anyone preached to the women in our church, they focused on either a submissive nature or the importance of a gentle and quiet spirit. I think it's plain to see that those things are very accurate descriptions of me. (That was an example of my sarcasm.) I heard 1 Peter 3:4 so many times I could recite it in my sleep: "You should clothe yourselves instead with the beauty that comes from within, the unfading beauty of a gentle and quiet spirit, which is so precious to God" (NLT). I was already struggling so hard in terms of my outer beauty, it seemed particularly important that I embrace the ideal of inner beauty. I felt especially pressured to assume "a gentle and quiet spirit" since I was longing to be found worthy, and these were the qualities that the leaders I admired esteemed and valued.

The girl I admired the most was my Bible study teacher. She was a few years older than me and just genuinely so sweet. She embodied everything

I thought a godly woman should look like, as though there were only one form and she had shaped the mold. Her whispery words dripped sweetness like honey, and I desperately wanted to be like her. I thought I could fake it till I made it, so I attempted to emulate the lilt of her voice and the way she punctuated her sentences with spiritual sounding phrases.

I'd heard that twenty-one days make a habit, so I spent twenty-one days in a row saying things like, "I had such a precious time with the Lord in my prayer closet this morning." But it was a totally failed experiment. For one thing, there was no room in my messy closet for me to pray in. For another, I don't think the whole twenty-one-day thing works on me. This is also why my bed is never made.

I kept trying to shape myself into the church girl persona, hoping it would be my ultimate transformation, sort of like when Cher and Dionne gave Tai a makeover in *Clueless* and then she became cool and confident. I thought if I peppered my speech with trendy Scripture references and doodled in the margins of my Bible with my scented glitter gel pens, I would naturally develop a gentle spirit as a result. *As if*. Needless to say, this didn't work either. It just served to make me feel inferior in my faith.

Mostly though, if I were to make an educated guess, I'd say my love of the nineties comes from the fact that it was the last decade in which my family was all together, before my parents' marriage imploded. I welcomed in the new millennium with my youth group friends in the church fellowship hall (where we all felt relatively safe from the dangers of Y2K), and then I went to live with my dad for my senior year of high school. It was a bittersweet year in my spiritual life, struggling under the strict ideals of my church but grateful for the refuge of a second family, even as my own was breaking apart. I felt displaced, split apart from my only sibling, and a bit lost as college loomed on the horizon. Life felt unsure and unstable, but the Bible study in that old barn never changed. It grounded me and gave me good friends. It gave me a place to go. Because of the church, I always had a spot on those overstuffed couches or crammed in the back of

Blake's beat-up blue Jeep. I don't know where I would have drifted off to if not for that tether.

———⤙

My husband once asked me if I regret those years, but I truly don't. I'm drawn to the heart of the church because it's where I first felt a sense of home. I keep returning there because homecomings are meant to be full of grace and mercy. I love the nineties, and I love the church.

In some ways, yes, I do think those years contributed to the shame in me, especially in how the focus was often more on our inequities rather than on how by His stripes we are healed.

But I think they also saved me, pulling me out of isolation and sending me searching for purpose. I think church is just like people, how sometimes we mean well and still manage to muck it all up.

So I refused to give up on it. Eventually I traded in my sparkly butterfly clips for wide-brimmed hats, and traded my well-worn teen study Bible for a grown-up one. I picked up a copy of *The Message* for a fresh look at ancient words I'd read so many times before. I found in the gospel of Matthew a verse I knew by heart, but one that had lost a bit of its luster for me around the same time I grew somewhat disenchanted with stained glass and steeples.

"Are you tired? Worn out? Burned out on religion? Come to me. Get away with me and you'll recover your life. I'll show you how to take a real rest. Walk with me and work with me—watch how I do it. Learn the unforced rhythms of grace. I won't lay anything heavy or ill fitting on you. Keep company with me and you'll learn to live freely and lightly." (Matt. 11:28–30 MSG)

Though I'm not even sure I knew it, this was what I was searching for. I wasn't tired of church. I was tired of all the striving. I had spent my life trying to earn my place—in my family, among my peers, and in heaven. Now I just wanted to rest. I was burned out on the dogma of religion, yearning for the pure simplicity of devotion. Parts of the faith I had known in the nineties had become "heavy" and "ill-fitting," kind of like that crop top I tried on in Target the other day. (The reemergence of nineties fashion in my thirties is still not a good look for me.) I wanted those "unforced rhythms of grace." I wanted to "live freely and lightly." I had wanted it to fit and it did, now that I let unbridled grace envelop me instead of trying to force it into a format.

"Get away with me . . . walk with me . . . work with me," the passage said. And so that's what I did. I had wanted to change the world for God, but what I found when I took a real rest was God changing *my* world. I got away with Him and I recovered my life. I didn't need to alter myself completely; I just needed to let the holiness of freedom coax out the hidden parts. Keeping company with God restored me.

When my first book was about to release, I was terrified my sense of humor might not translate well. It tends to be a bit dry, which is really just more evidence that I was meant to be British. Yet interestingly, as feedback came in, people's fondness for the sarcasm was a common thread. They liked it. I was completely shocked, but I guess it makes sense. It was the overflow of learning to live freely and lightly and authentically.

And besides, I'm apparently much better in writing.

CHAPTER 10

Inside Out

The most important kind of freedom is to be what
you really are. . . . There can't be any large-scale
revolution until there's a personal revolution, on an
individual level. It's got to happen inside first.
—Jim Morrison

Every morning the sleek silver alarm clock sitting on my
husband's nightstand goes off, waking us up to the tune of whatever is
playing on the local radio station to which I synced it. I enjoy the spon-
taneity in not knowing what song I will awaken to each morning, like my
own little game of alarm clock roulette.

Early on in our marriage I discovered that unlike me, my husband is
not a morning person. I made this discovery when our trusty alarm clock
woke us up to a jaunty little tune by the Red Hot Chili Peppers. I threw
off the bed covers and sang along enthusiastically. He reached over clum-
sily and mashed the snooze button, effectively cutting off both myself and
Anthony Keidis. "Jeff, why would you not wake up and sing along to that
song?" I asked incredulously. He put a pillow over his head and mumbled,
"Why would you ever wake up singing anything at all?" Clearly we are
soul mates.

Personally, my ideal morning would start like a scene out of a Disney
movie, whereupon I would throw open the curtains to be surrounded by
a bevy of woodland creatures who would help me with my daily chores as
I frittered about my house describing my actions in song. My husband's

ideal morning doesn't even begin until at least 10 a.m. Even then he would prefer silence for the next half hour as he slowly powers on for the day, like a vintage computer. Do you even know how many words I need to say out loud by 10:30 in the morning?

All of them.

I need to say all of the words.

This is why my daughter sometimes wanders into the kitchen to find me talking to myself while peeling vegetables and asks with a sigh, "Mommy, are you talking invisible again?"

In the first weeks after our wedding, I found myself feeling hurt and confused by Jeff's post-work routine, which involved more alone time than I had anticipated. I thought maybe after living with me for a little bit, he'd determined for himself the very thing I was secretly afraid of: that I was too much. I don't mean "too much" in the way people say it as a compliment, like, "Oh, you are just too much!" I mean as in maybe having me in his life was overwhelming, like in a "this is more than I bargained for" sort of sense.

Then one day I stumbled upon his little secret: my husband is an introvert. He doesn't hate coming home to *me*; he just needs space to decompress and reset after a long day at work being surrounded by other people. I have no idea what this is like on account of how I *love* being surrounded by other people. That's the whole reason I got married in the first place. For the constant company. (Also for the making out. But mostly the company.)

It is a sacred work to shape two separate personalities around one another to inhabit a home. It's not just the way we bump up against one another, our energies all bound between four walls and a roof, but how vulnerable each of us must be to entangle our souls. It takes a knowing, an unveiling of our own self to our own self and before each other. The intimacy is in the Eden nakedness of it all, every bit of us on display and trusting the other with the whole of it, body and soul.

You learn a lot about the person you married when you begin cohabiting with them. For example, I learned that guys get hair all over the bathroom when they shave. A decade later and I am still constantly sweeping beard hair off my baseboards. My husband learned that sometimes when I'm washing my face at night, I like to pretend I'm in a Neutrogena commercial. He's all, "Why are you smiling at yourself in the mirror like that?" (Admittedly I did not mean for him to walk in on me that one time.)

I learned that he always has to sleep on the left side of the bed. He learned that I abhor using a fork and prefer to eat everything that isn't pasta with a tiny spoon. I learned that he gets eerily quiet when he's angry. He learned that I get passionately upset about things he does in my dreams. (I cannot help this. I'm just a girl, standing in front of a boy, ranting irrationally about something he did in my dream last night.)

But the real education is in exposing *yourself* so wholly to another person that you can't avoid the parts of yourself you'd rather keep hidden. Sometimes to make a marriage, you have to unmake yourself by abandoning the armor you've amassed after past rejections and go all in, unguarded.

Sometimes you have to strip everything down to bare to find out who you really are.

I took my first personality test in college, a Myers-Briggs test because that's one of the requirements when you claim sociology as your major. I've taken many more tests since, because I am overly fascinated with personality and human relationships. Also because I'm a bit of a geek and enjoy reading detailed personality profiles.

So I knew a lot of about my personality type before I even got married, like how I'm an ENFP (high in Extraversion, Intuition, Feeling, Perception) and, according to The Color Quiz, an Orange. This essentially means I have a lot of feelings that I need to express constantly.

It's possible that Scarlette may have inherited these traits from me. The reason I think so is because we have a new babysitter coming today, and Scarlette is currently standing at the door bouncing up and down yelling, "I'm going to tell her all about EVERYTHING! Everything that I know I am going to tell her!" (I'm over here thinking, *Godspeed, new babysitter. Godspeed.*)

I recently completed the questionnaire at www.16personalities.com, and as I went through the detailed synopsis, I began to feel overwhelmed at how chillingly accurate the description was. I may have even worried for a moment that someone had slipped miniature spy cameras into my house—one, because I'm so extremely logical and, two, because my husband has forced me to watch one too many conspiracy theory movies. (The things we do for love.)

According to the test I took, only 7 percent of the population falls into my particular category. So, okay, this did sort of give credence to my lifelong thought that maybe I'm a bit different. And sure, 7 percent seems like a pretty small number. But with approximately 6 billion people in the world, that means there are about 420 million people out there like me. I'm bound to run into a kindred spirit every now and again. If life were like *Harry Potter*, I would be sorted into a house with my like-minded peers.

(Ravenclaw, according to the quiz I just took online.)

Since I spent my college years studying things like nature vs. nurture, I am ever watchful also of my own children's developing personalities. One of the best parts of having children is getting to perform sociological observations on them. (I know. I'm a blast to have at parties.) Scarlette, for instance, is boisterous and affectionate and loves an audience. Like me, she has a lot of feelings. Just earlier today I told her to "stop giving me a sassy face," and she replied very seriously, "Mommy. I am NOT sassy face-ing you. I am just having some feelings about dis wif my EYES."

Along these lines, my husband and I decided to take her to see the movie *Inside Out*, because Pixar never goes wrong with a movie and because of my slight obsession with Amy Poehler, who narrates the movie as its main character, the emotion Joy, animated as a tiny glittering spark with bright blue hair. The film's premise is that human personalities are made up of core memories, events that are so impactful they shape who we become. So in the movie, core memories are formed through a mingling of emotions—the bright yellow of Joy tinged with the glowing blue of Sadness. They're complex, the colors swirling together to define what makes us each unique. The whole concept, beyond being cute and entertaining, does leave an impression.

Not too many days later, Scarlette and I were out shopping and passed a girl dressed all in black except with bright blue hair and about fifteen facial piercings. Scarlette broke free from my hand and ran over to her. I got nervous and clammy because I was sure she was about to barrage this girl with questions about the small silver chain that connected the ring in her nose to the ring in her lip. Instead, Scarlette beamed at her and said, "Excuse me, miss, I LOVE your hair. You look just like Joy!" (I love the way Scarlette sees the world, because that girl was absolutely dressed like the Grim Reaper.)

In her short five years, Scarlette's colors are mostly a cheerful, sparkling yellow. She is all joy. Because she has not yet been introduced to shame.

———————✦

My friend Lauren told me she was insecure about the sensitive part of her personality. "I was basically taught that being sensitive, anxious, or depressed is a character flaw," she said, "and that I should just snap or pray my way out of it." When we open up our vulnerabilities, we find our kindred people. "Co-sign," I wrote her back.

Sensitivity was frowned upon in my upbringing as well. Among the refrains often uttered at me through pursed lips was "Don't be such a baby," accompanied by a disapproving look that seems as genetic as blue eyes in our family line. Even now I occasionally catch myself feeling that same sharp look beginning to form, and I hastily hurry to rearrange my facial features before my eyes narrow in the direction of my offspring.

If I look back over my family tree, I see it snaking over the branches on my mother's side—the unspoken, unyielding expectation for women to be ever put-together, a perfectly lined stiff upper lip. Being sensitive had no place in such sturdy stock. We were not women who were weak-willed.

When my mother unraveled her childhood in a therapist's office, she could see this same serpent of deception, coiled and poised to strike. It looked like a family friend intruding on a little girl's innocence, and it hissed an admonishment to keep it quiet for everyone else's sake but hers. It brought with it shame that solidified into a frigid anger. That's how the fruit of a tree becomes bitter, when it's left unprotected from the frostbite. You can try to bury shame deep down below, but it will seep into the roots. Then when the dam breaks, it will upend the forest and ravage the village. My self-confidence was damaged in the wake.

One of my girlfriends told me a story about how when she was a little girl, she desperately wanted to impress her mother, a renowned singer. She waited until she was within earshot of her mom and then started softly singing to herself, hoping for some kind of affirmation, knowing musicality was something her mother valued highly. Instead, her mother criticized her for being off-key. My friend tells me she never sang in front of her mother again.

We're all just searching for someone's approval. Longing for acceptance. We're trying to prove something to somebody, and it keeps us striving, never granting us rest. When we chase validation instead of sanctification, we never find a reprieve from our own self-doubt.

It's an excruciating thing to seek acceptance where it should be given freely, and it's a freeing thing to find an everlasting acceptance that doesn't have to be sought.

I have learned since to embrace the beauty in each unique personality instead of finding flaws or faults or failures. To take people as they are. I looked for my mother's "well done" as she had looked for her mother's before her, and she her mother's before that. You can't keep a tree healthy without pruning, cutting back the afflicted spots so new life can grow. This is the work we're doing now, my mother and I, nurturing the tiny shoots of life that make up the next generation. It's a laborious remaking, a rebuilding, but the thing about God is that even when you burn it all down, He is quite capable at restoring from ashes. So we're finding new words and we're weaving them together to cover our children and our grandchildren in love. We're allowing the colors to mingle, the happiness to exist with sadness.

We are living out the transformation.

We are working in grace.

One of my favorite books is *The Five Love Languages* by Gary Chapman. It's been so helpful in helping assess my personality type and recognize the ways I give and receive love. Seeing my personality defined from afar without judgment has showed me so many positive attributes in myself that I had simply misunderstood. What I thought was too sensitive was actually empathy; what I thought was an overflow of extroversion was actually the blessing of exhortation. Understanding myself has been crucial to learning to love myself, as well as to believing that I was created with a sacred sort of purposeful love.

As a result of this, as I've gotten older, I've just decided to embrace certain parts of my personality rather than continue nursing the shame that's been so often attached to them. This is likely what people mean when they talk about "with age comes wisdom" and all that. One of these traits is my tendency to frequently find myself in awkward situations. You know the saying "If you run into a jerk in the morning, you ran into a jerk. If you run into jerks all day, you are the jerk." Replace "jerk" with "awkward person," and that's me in a nutshell.

After my first book released, I learned that doing a bunch of radio interviews is part of the process of publishing a book. Speaking from a rehearsed script is something I can manage. Speaking off the cuff live on the air, however, is not my forte. I learned this fact about myself when I was speaking live on the air for the first time. It was really great timing for this sort of revelation.

I recorded many of the interviews over Skype, and I did my best to appear author-ly and professional. The interviewers couldn't see I was wearing pajama pants, but from the waist up I thought I looked the part. I did about a month's worth of these podcast interviews before I noticed that underneath my photograph was a little "About Me" section that lit up whenever I was live. I guess I'd filled it in years before when I was binge-watching one of my favorite television shows, *The Office*. It read, "I wear doll clothes."

I am so good at making first impressions.

The worst part was that I didn't even have it credited as a quote from the TV series, so I'm sure every one of the legitimate journalists who interviewed me thought I was less "professional author" and more "eccentric writer-ly type." Or possibly they just assumed I was exceptionally small, like Thumbelina.

Awkward? Undoubtedly. But now I simply embrace the positive things that flow from my awkwardness. Unashamed. I choose to see it as a blessing to other people. Because, I figure, if I'm the awkward one in an interaction, it probably leaves them feeling pretty good about their own social skills. It's a nice little confidence boost for them, plus they get an interesting story to tell their families around the dinner table that night. They've just learned a good lesson, for example, about what not to say when you're buying feminine products and get flustered at the counter. Really I'm providing a valuable service to society, if you think about it.

Awkward or sensitive or joyful or having a lot of feelings with your eyes, every bit of it is purposeful. Every bit of it has been given as a way for us to exude God's glory, hope, and redemption to the outside world. And we can learn to believe it if we'll just allow ourselves to look closer at where the colors mingle. Because "the LORD has made everything for its purpose" (Prov. 16:4 ESV). "For we are his workmanship" (Eph. 2:10 ESV).

CHAPTER 11

Thief of Joy

Comparison is the thief of joy.
Theodore Roosevelt

Whenever I need a little levity in my life, I text my little sister. "Hey, I'm having writer's block. Tell me some funny stories about our childhood that I can use in this book," I wrote her. She texted back in rapid-fire succession:

> What about the time I got mad at you and tore the bottom right corners out of your latest *Anne of Green Gables* novel so you couldn't finish each page?
>
> Or that time I put a piece of baloney in your CD player and then blamed the bad smell on the fact that you never cleaned your room?
>
> Oh, or that one time I lit all your candles and then threw the lit match in your trash can and caught your room on fire?

"I said *funny* stories, you little sociopath."

My sister was born five years after me, and I took to her with a tender affection as she toddled around behind me, all towheaded and mischievous. She let me dress her up in outrageous outfits and would do just about anything I told her to. I pretty much abandoned all of my Cabbage Patch Kids in favor of this little doll-child who had come to life. I was fiercely protective of her, and the only fight I've ever been in happened on our elementary school playground when I punched a girl right in the mouth for making her cry.

Then we grew up.

One year around Christmastime I spotted the most perfect accessory a girl in the early nineties could ever want—an acid-washed denim bean-bag covered in neon paint splatters. I put it on my Christmas list every single year for the next three years until finally the time came. At the very end of our Christmas celebration, when all of the gifts had been opened and exclaimed over, my grandparents declared there was one gift left. This was it. This was my Red Ryder BB gun moment, like when Ralphie's dad hid his coveted Christmas gift behind the tree. My grandmother walked out with an acid-washed, neon paint splattered beanbag. I squealed. Then she presented it with a flourish. To my sister.

It was basically just like that story in the Bible where Jacob steals Esau's birthright.

As I entered my awkward tween years, my affection turned to envy. The sibling rivalry was strong, made worse by the way we each felt pigeon-holed into our familial roles. I was the smart one; she was the pretty one. I was the shy one; she was the outgoing one.

She was my opposite in every way. Her hair was sleek and blonde, where mine was mouse brown and fuzzy. She was vibrant and extroverted, whereas I was timid and mercurial. She sported a sun-kissed glow as she cartwheeled across the sand, while I sat slathered in SPF 500 that came out of the tube as white as my skin. My jealousy only intensified as we grew older. I felt as though she was the culmination of the best traits of my parents, and I had somehow managed to get a combination of all the undesirable ones, like I was some sort of faulty prototype and she was the polished final draft.

Then she tested into gifted classes, and it turned out she was smart too. That was, like, the only thing I had left. A girl could see how Joseph's brothers might want to ditch him in the desert. That's why I left her stranded in a tree one day when we were playing in the woods behind our house. Replace "coat of many colors" with "splatter-painted beanbag," and it's pretty much the same story.

People loved my sister, and it wasn't just imagined. We could hardly leave the house without someone comparing her to Jon Benet Ramsey, the infamous miniature beauty queen. Once when a pizza delivery guy spotted a framed Glamour Shot photo of my sister and me, circa 1992, hanging on my wall in sight of the doorway, he asked how I knew her.

"That's my sister," I told him wearily.

"Your sister is Jon Benet Ramsey?" he exclaimed. Then I found a new place to order pizza from.

She was better at telling stories than me too. They weren't true, but they were better. Like this one time when she framed a picture of Michael J. Fox, took it to show-and-tell, and told everyone he was our uncle—pretty convincingly, it turned out, made even more so by the fact that our last name was, in fact, Fox. This set off a string of events in which the PTA president asked my mom if her brother would be willing to come speak to our elementary school. Initially she acquiesced, not thinking it such a far-fetched request since her actual brother was serving in the Air Force at the time. Up until that little yarn came all unraveled, my sister had everyone charmed.

Then there was gymnastics. My hand-eye coordination has never been anything to write home about, but in gymnastics I found my niche. I practiced back hip circles on our rickety backyard swing set, persistent and determined. I advanced quickly through the levels, and it was the first time I felt confident and accomplished and proud.

Then *she* started in gymnastics, wanting to be like her big sister. Only she had the benefit of natural athleticism on her side and was soon ranking just behind me. I side-eyed her from my perch on the beam, watching her tumble across the floor when I slipped and fell and crumbled. I didn't make an impressive comeback à la Kerri Strug in the '96 Olympics. I limped off to the side, bitter and broken.

In many ways we were made better because we drew off one another's energy, and we could have been iron sharpening iron, if only I hadn't let envy dull my edge. Instead I quit, choosing to sit on the sidelines rather than watch my little sister surpass me and share the spotlight. I gave up on something I loved just because I was afraid of being relegated to second best. She was warm and vivacious and funny and beautiful and talented. No matter what I did, I always felt as though I was living in the shadow of my little sister.

So pretty much, I was the Ashlee to her Jessica Simpson. Which is ironic because my sister all grown up actually looks just like Ashlee Simpson. Recently a friend walked past the wedding pictures hanging in my hallway and did a double take because she thought Ashlee Simpson was my maid of honor.

(I seriously need to frame some different pictures of my sister.)

Ever since the creation of humankind, we have wanted what isn't ours—Eve in the center of a Garden, David in a clandestine affair born from a lingering glance on a rooftop. Envy is at the heart of a dozen or more stories in the Bible: brother slain by brother; a rainbow-colored coat; a woman in the kitchen, envious of her sister at Jesus' feet. Although apparently in biblical times, people were pretty extreme about it. I never wanted to maim my little sister; I just wanted some of her accolades for myself. Envy suffocated me.

In Georgia we have this plant called kudzu, a creeping vine that winds its way up the limbs of a tree until it eventually covers it completely, blocking out the light and choking out the life. When I want to find solace, I drive east toward the mountains on a small, winding road that cuts a path through the forest. I'm surrounded by trees draped in kudzu, casting odd-shaped shadows on the pavement. You cannot see the tree itself; the vine is a thief that has stolen its shape. It looks like a tree, tall and thriving, yet it's dying inside the shell of itself. It is one thing on the outside, and another on the inside.

And this is what envy does to us, creeps up slowly until we're trapped inside ourselves, withering from lack of light. It robs us of our relationships and of our own potential. Ecclesiastes 4:4 notes, "Then I observed that most people are motivated to success because they envy their neighbors. But this, too, is meaningless—like chasing the wind" (Eccles. 4:4 NLT). It's a futile pursuit.

Jeff and I were walking along a park trail when we came across a set of metal bars. "Look! They have gymnastic bars!" I exclaimed delightedly. "That's kind of a weird thing to have in the middle of a park though. Like, who comes to the park to flip around the bars?"

That's when my sweet husband informed me they were actually chin-up bars, which does make a bit more sense, and also accurately represents just how often I work out. "I bet I can totally still do a back hip circle. Spot me," I instructed him, over his profuse objections. I'm praying about his lack of faith in me.

I swung my body up and over the bar and flipped around three times in succession. I could tell my husband was pretty impressed . . . until he had to half carry me back to the car, because apparently I'm way too old for this sort of thing. I also might have a slight problem with pride. I thought about the smell of a chalk-filled gym and the bend of the bars under my weight. I thought about the years when my sister and I were distant. I thought about what could have been.

There were plenty of things in my life I could have enjoyed if I had just been able to focus on my own portion rather than someone else's. Instead, I spent my energy comparing myself relentlessly to an imagined version of myself. I allowed envy to erode something sacred in our sisterhood. This is what envy always does to relationships, throwing them into chaos because "where there is envy and selfish ambition, there is disorder" (James 3:16). I could have celebrated my sister instead of harboring resentment. I could have been her biggest cheerleader. I could have written a better story for us.

Luckily another thing that my sister is very good at is not holding grudges.

———⤙

I love going apple picking in the fall. Maybe it's the nostalgia of my youth, or maybe it's the fact that fresh-made apple cider is like my personal ambrosia, but hand on heart I look forward to the local apple festival every year almost as much as I look forward to my birthday. Autumn is my favorite season because of corn mazes and bonfires and apple picking. I also love pumpkin spice lattes, oversized sweaters, and riding boots. I might be a little bit basic.

Every fall I see pictures of happy families posing in orchards as I scroll through my newsfeed. My introverted husband does not share my love of spending the day in a crowd of people picking our own apples. Sometimes he accompanies me anyhow because of marital compromise. Like how I agreed to hang a massive television over our fireplace instead of the oversized faux magnolia wreath I'd been eyeing, and he agreed to take me to a real, live pumpkin patch, despite his wondering why we couldn't just "buy one out of those bins in the grocery store."

It never fails that every fall on Facebook, my friends post pretty pictures of their families out apple picking. Sometimes I feel a little irked that their husbands look happy to be hanging out in an orchard, as though maybe they didn't even have to compromise for it. In the digital landscape in which we live, it's easier than ever to find our thoughts slipping from celebration to comparison.

The setting for my work is on the Internet, and I owe that space tremendously for giving an audience to my words. The one thing every aspiring writer wants is someone to read what they've written. I love what I do, but I have to be constantly conscious that much of what I see online is carefully curated. Even Christian culture can't escape the social pressure of presenting an artfully arranged life on the Internet. There's the perfectly posed passage of Scripture next to an artisanal cup of coffee. A pink bouquet of peonies in a manicured hand. Sometimes I scroll through Instagram and feel like the modern church was infiltrated by an Anthropologie catalog. It kind of feels like a sorority that we're not a part of. It's just that this time instead of a lunchroom, it's a farmhouse table and flower crowns.

When we arrange our lives into snapshots, no one gets the whole picture. Confession: I never read the Bible surrounded by bouquets of wildflowers. I have the Bible open in front of me right now, for instance, and to my left is a diaper pail that seriously needs to be emptied. And if I were to zoom out on this frame, you'd see the pile of laundry I've been meaning to fold for the past three days. (Okay, fine, for the past three weeks.) If there's anything I've learned in this line of work, it's that every-thing viewed through a screen has a bias. I carefully crop my still frames to conceal my mess. The only time my house looks perfect is on the Internet. I share the essence of things, but not always the soul of them. We are never truly seeing someone's one hundred percent. I know this . . . and yet still I have to be cautious of comparing.

I read an article the other day that talked about comparison and the phrase "I can't hold a candle to her."

In the days of apprenticeship, of hierarchy and social caste sys-tems and manual labor, to hold the candle of a more experienced workman while they chiseled, wrote, and labored overnight was an honor. It was the duty of a trusted apprentice, a helper. It was one person offering time and appreciation to another. It was deep respect. *I see you have a gift. Here, let me help you offer it to the world.* To not hold a candle to someone else, then, has little to do with comparison. It isn't a sign of a lower status, a lesser person with lesser gifts. It's simply choosing not to encourage another. It's being unwilling to help them labor through the night. It's us, sitting in the dark, saying, who them? They're brilliant? Why would they need my help? And that's where we all stay, then. Dimly lit, cold. Not holding candles to one another.[1]

We waste a relationship if we spend it comparing rather than light bearing.

We could glean so much wisdom from the women in our lives if we stepped out from our own shadows of shame. I learned how to baby wear and cook dry beans from Florica. I told her I wanted to cook from scratch like she did, and so she busied herself in my kitchen before the cancer took her. I'm so grateful that when I mentioned what I admired, she offered to let me hold a candle. I think of her whenever I make chili, how she let me come alongside her and learn her crafts.

As my friends and I talked about what kept us from developing good relationships, comparison kept coming up as one of the biggest inhibitors. "I compare myself to what I see others doing," my friend Kelly said. "I think, *She must be so smart or so healthy or such an amazing mom*. It keeps me from becoming acquainted with someone because I've already judged myself as not measuring up."

I'm guilty of it, too, looking at what other women are doing and then trying to incorporate those things into my life. In my head, I think changing myself to be more like someone else is going to make me a well-rounded woman, living a more beautifully balanced life. But in reality, it just leads to me being spread too thin, trying to accomplish things that aren't even in my area of gifting, rather than giving my best to what I do well. Instead of feeling adept and confident, I just feel like a failure at everything in a negative cycle of my own making.

We don't have to do what someone else is doing to be considered worthy. Likewise, we don't have to undercut someone else's good fortune for fear that it will steal away our own. We are never going to feel better about ourselves by tearing others down. As the apostle Paul liked to say, "Let each person examine his own work, and then he can take pride in himself alone, and not compare himself with someone else" (Gal. 6:4). I think we can look at the good things our friends are doing, and instead of feeling like we need to measure up to them, we can champion them on, knowing that what is good for them is not necessarily for us. "That is the motto that women should constantly repeat over and over again. Good for her! Not for me."[2] (That's right. I just quoted Amy Poehler to make my point about the Bible. Scripture is everywhere, folks.)

We don't have to feel attacked by other people's accomplishments.

We can make our comparison a compliment.

We can hold a candle.

CHAPTER 12

Measuring Up

The worry of what others are doing or are expecting us
to do will indeed kill our souls. Even worse, it separates
us from God's voice, the only voice that truly matters.
—Sarah Mae

For some reason, probably because I'm so incredibly logical, I just assumed after I got married that I would become skilled in all things domestic and housewifery. I'm not exactly sure how I thought this transition would come about, being that just one week before I got married I burned a microwaveable cup of Easy Mac. I suppose I thought the act of sliding on a wedding ring held some sort of ancient magic that would suddenly make me good at things like ironing and cooking and remembering to vacuum. Spoiler alert: it did not. Turns out, wedding rings do not work like the ones in *The Hobbit*.

So it came as quite a surprise to me after the wedding to discover that although I was a married woman, I was still a terrible housekeeper and an even worse cook. And if you thought it surprised *me*, you should have seen my husband's reaction. I don't think he quite grasped the extent of just how messy I can be, mostly because I kept him out of my disaster of a bedroom when we were dating under the guise of not wanting him to see my wedding dress. Which was not technically a lie. I really didn't want him to see my wedding dress. I just also did not want him to see the 639 piles of dirty laundry surrounding said wedding dress. I like to call this sort of omission "using my words with finesse."

The worst revelation, though, was how terrible I was in the kitchen. I feel as though cooking and writing are skills that seem to go hand in hand. Mostly because of the very scientific observations I've made by reading books. Lately every book I read seems to include some sort of original recipe. I read a devotional book a few weeks ago, and nestled right there in the middle of the daily devotions was a recipe for homemade focaccia bread. I'm sorry to tell you that you will not find any recipes in these pages, unless you count that one story about the time I decided to stuff my bra with Jell-O pudding-filled balloons. That was most definitely a recipe. For disaster.

Prior to getting married, I never had to plan out and cook meals. The closest I ever came to making a gourmet meal for two was microwaving water from the bathroom tap in our college dorm room and pouring it over ramen noodles to split with my roommate. What I miss the most about college isn't the late-night pizza parties in the dorm or the lazy afternoons on the quad. It's the fact that three times a day I could walk into the cafeteria and get a delicious hot meal that I didn't have to cook or clean up after. Meal plans were a great blessing in my life. Guess you never know how good you've got it.

I remember my husband and I discussing my dislike of cooking when we were engaged, declaring my insistence that I would enjoy it when we were married. "Then I'll be cooking as a *wife*. It will be, like, my *job*," I told him emphatically. It's so cute how naïve I was. I truly believed that once we said, "I do," I would be blessed with Martha Stewart-esque domestic skills and that I would count it all joy because that's what I'd been taught about biblical womanhood.

So you can see how it was slightly confusing to me when I felt less like counting it all joy and more like throwing my spatula across the room the sixth time I burnt our dinner black. My husband insisted he'd be happy to cook a few nights a week because he actually enjoyed it. I resisted his efforts to help because I thought it would diminish my worth as a woman.

If I couldn't get dinner on the table in some sort of edible fashion, I felt like a total failure as a wife.

Why did I decide that was the measure of my worth as a woman?

What happened, I think, is that once upon a time someone read Proverbs 31 and decided then and there to make its list of accomplishments the measuring stick for married women. From that day on, it became a go-to resource for anyone preaching to women and a source of constant irritation for girls like me who felt enormous pressure to live up to it.

I sat through countless sermons that defined womanhood by an ability to accomplish household tasks from Old Testament times. Women's events at church were titled things like "How to Become a Proverbs 31 Woman" and often emphasized the portion of the passage that mentioned how such a woman was never idle. This did not bode well for my love of Netflix.

A kind, older woman once gave me a book based on this passage of Scripture as a wedding gift, which (among its many practical applications) instructed me to meet my husband at the door each evening with a quiet voice and fresh makeup. It also recommended that I change out of any clothes the baby may have spit up on, in order to greet my husband with a pleasant appearance. The closest I ever came to meeting my husband with a pleasant appearance after having a baby was the day he found me in the buff, due to the fact that the baby had just thrown up on all of my available clothing. But I don't think that's exactly what the book meant.

The only thing in Proverbs 31 that I was even remotely adept at was verse 15: "She rises while it is still night and provides food for her household." And that wasn't even by choice so much as being a byproduct of a baby who woke up every two hours in the middle of the night to nurse. (Also, according to verse 15 she apparently has a whole bunch of servants. Listen, I could make my own linens too if I had live-in household help is all I'm saying.)

Without having a framework that focused on the hopefulness in the writing, I imagined this legendary portrait of a woman as something completely unattainable. Probably like you did. But when I learned that the original intent of Proverbs 31 was not meant as a list of tasks to check off but as a way to encourage women in their femininity, it completely changed the way I felt about that passage of Scripture for the better. In fact, I discovered that in Jewish culture, it is the men who memorize this particular passage of Scripture in order to sing it to their wives as a blessing over a Sabbath meal.[1]

I had to pause my research right there. I practically skipped downstairs to let my husband know that I had an excellent idea of how to improve our meal times. I have no idea why he did not immediately get on board with the thought of serenading me over dinner.

Then I learned that some scholars believe that Proverbs 31 is not referencing a single woman at all, but is instead an amalgamation of desirable character traits. An inspirational character, much like how the Proverbs refer to Wisdom as a *she*. In fact, the very first verse of the chapter begins, "The words of King Lemuel, a pronouncement that his mother taught him." What follows, they say, is King Lemuel's mother using the Hebrew alphabet to list out character attributes he should seek out in a wife, which means that the Proverbs 31 passage was written as an acrostic poem. That's the type of poem where the first word of each sentence begins with a specific letter. Have you ever tried to write an acrostic poem? It's really hard. For example:

Knock-kneed

Always running late

Young and restless

Lover of lattes

Author of poorly written acrostics

Admittedly I have a first name that includes some of the worst possible letters to get in a game of Scrabble but still, acrostics are hard. Major props to the king's mom for pulling that off so well. (Personally I prefer the art of the haiku.)

I loved learning to reframe that chapter of Scripture as a blessing, allowing it to name the value in me and the virtue in my work. Without the binding constraints of chastisement that I had so often heard in the preaching of those verses, I was able to fully embrace the beauty in the poetry. As a writer and a wannabe homemaker, I love reading the Proverbs as artfully written biblical literature, rather than as a lofty list of chores.

For a long time I thought that if I could just keep house well, I'd be closer to being that ever elusive picture of the Proverbs 31 woman. This new shift in perspective has made all the difference in the renewing of my mind and setting me on the path toward spiritual freedom. When I'm not weighed down by the burden of trying to achieve someone else's standards, I am free to live with the spirit of virtue that Proverbs 31 extols. I am emboldened in my womanhood because I draw my strength from my Creator, not my skills. Instead of feeling daunted, I am dauntless.

Which is what I need to find my center.

And also because the pile of pots and pans in my sink has been there for three days and will take a great act of bravery, resilience, and possibly a HAZMAT suit to conquer.

———✦———

On a shelf in my kitchen sits my favorite set of measuring cups, a dainty, white collection shaped like flowers with hand-painted floral scenes scrolling intricately across the handles. They are delicate and fragile and all together ineffectual at their intended purpose. I never use them to measure anything because they are absolutely worthless as measuring cups. Instead I reach for the sturdy steel set that never chips or spills or randomly breaks off in my hand at the handle. They're made from sturdier stock, and I know exactly where I stand with them. They're like the Rick Astley of measuring cups. They are never, ever going to let me down.

I'm a girl who loves comedy. My secret dream is to be on *Saturday Night Live*. My fictional kindred spirit is Leslie Knope, from *Parks and Recreation*, so I was excited to watch an interview with Amy Poehler, who happens to be one of my favorite comedians. The male host, Neal Brennan, was confiding to her how he feels it's difficult to meet the societal expectations of being a modern man.

Amy (I like to pretend we're on a first-name basis) looked amused as she responded, "Well, this feeling that you're having right now, which is like, 'I'm supposed to be all things,' is a feeling that women have every day and have their whole lives."[2]

Then I kind of fist-pumped the air in solidarity, which was awkward since I was sitting in the waiting room of my dentist's office. It wasn't just trying to live up to the mishandling of a chapter in Proverbs that had exhausted me. In our current culture, women are under so much pressure to be all things while simultaneously being told not to be too much of the things. Be sexy, but not sexual. Speak up, but quietly, don't be bossy. And always smile. It is no wonder we feel like we don't measure up. The current standard of measurement is impossible to reach. We don't need to take on more tasks. We don't need to measure up. We just need a new measuring stick.

After graduation from high school, I noticed the girls in our church circles were being referred to by a new name. And it wasn't "recent graduates" or "college bound," despite the fact that the majority of us were headed for higher education. It was Ladies In Waiting.

I'm not being facetious. Sadly, this had nothing to do with how to become Princess Kate's right-hand woman and instead was designed as a means of preparing us girls to become godly wives. We were told it was important to become God's best while we waited for Mister Right.

The latter half of that premise makes me cringe a bit, now that I have a daughter of my own. Kathleen Norris said, "I wonder if children don't begin to reject both poetry and religion for similar reasons, because the way both are taught takes the life out of them."[3] It seems like our girls might be better served if we taught them that they could become their best selves without impressing on them the idea that their faith journey can only be counted worthwhile if it sets them on the path to a husband. More importantly, what if we declined to insinuate that worth and waiting went hand in hand, as though we needed to be more prepared to be a spouse than a saint?

What if we were just faithfully *living*? What if we weren't filling a time "in between"? What if we stayed fully entrenched in a life spent following the Lord, one that could be *complemented* by a husband, of course, but wouldn't be left with a hopeless void for the lack of one? I think our girls would be so much more empowered to explore their God-given gifts if their walk with Christ wasn't endeavoring to lead them down the aisle.

I fear we often bandy about the term "freedom" while subsequently spiritually enslaving our girls to a prescribed ideal of womanhood. Our identities are not defined by our responsibilities. We are more than just our roles. We are more than who we are in the waiting.

I don't think I'm the only one who feels this way because I read *Cold Tangerines* by Shauna Niequist and felt this statement resonate so deeply:

> I have always, essentially, been waiting. Waiting to become something else, waiting to be that person I always thought I was on the verge of becoming, waiting for that life I thought I would have. In my head, I was always one step away. In high school, I was biding my time until I could become the college version of myself, the one my mind could see so clearly. In college, the post-college "adult" person was always looming in front of me, smarter, stronger, more organized. . . . And through all that waiting, here I am. My life is passing, day by day, and I am waiting

for it to start. I am waiting for that time, that person, that event when my life will finally begin.[4]

Or maybe it's just me and Shauna Niequist who feel that way, in which case we should really hang out, but I think our culture has conditioned us to always be waiting for the next best thing, the next best version of ourselves.

As a woman, you can barely pass into one stage of life without someone asking you about the next. If you're dating, you'll be asked when you're getting married. If you're married, they'll want to know when the babies are coming. When you have a baby, they'll want to know when you're having another. (But don't have too many because once you pass a certain threshold, people start asking things like, "Don't you know how that happens?") We are measured by meeting milestones that are others-centric, and this creates a tension and a striving, always trying to reach the next rung on the ladder. I don't think this is what God intended for the woman fashioned from dust and rib.

A single year in our lives is measured in five hundred, twenty five thousand, six hundred minutes. I know this fact because of my fondness for musical theater. The earth makes its loop around the sun, and I hang up a new calendar on the wall above my desk, next to the pinboard full of pictures of the people I love. This is how I want my life measured, not by the state of my kitchen or the size of my thigh gap, but by the legacies I leave in my words and my works. What I want for my daughter, for generations of girls, is to know they are more than their roles and responsibilities. What I want you to know, for you as a woman, is that your worth isn't determined by your standing adjacent to other people. We are made worthy by redemption and that isn't something we earn or attain. It's just a gift.

———⟶

Whenever I watch Scarlette play, I think about how free she is. Her innocence makes me want a faith that is childlike because it is boundless and unrestrained.

Free.

In Isaiah 61 we read, "He has sent me to heal the brokenhearted, to proclaim liberty to the captives and freedom to the prisoners" (v. 1). This was God's promise to actual prisoners, that they would be free from their captivity, but it is also a promise to us, that in Christ we are liberated from what has kept us caged. Our shame, our insecurities, our doubt. Because God is in the generous work of redemption, He trades it all for joy. "In place of your shame, you will have a double portion; in place of disgrace, they will rejoice over their share. So they will possess double in their land, and eternal joy will be theirs" (Isa. 61:7).

I don't know what life holds for Scarlette, but I know my goal as her mother is to inspire her to embrace a spirit of freedom rather than shame. If I can live this way, she'll have a better chance at warding off the pressures and expectations and messages that will inundate her as she grows into womanhood. If each of us communicates worth instead of shame to our girls, then one by one they'll grow up into a generation of women who, like Isaiah 61, are set free. And so maybe we weren't so far off the mark in the nineties after all.

Maybe that's how we change the world.

CHAPTER 13

For Such a Time as This

> "I wish it need not have happened in my time," said Frodo.
> "So do I," said Gandalf, "and so do all who live to see
> such times. But that is not for them to decide. All we have
> to decide is what to do with the time that is given us."
> —J. R. R. Tolkien

When I'm in the middle of a writing project, it's not unusual to find notes I've written to myself in random places all over our house. I'm always jotting down little phrases or ideas I don't want to forget. The whole reason I keep a dry-erase marker in the bathroom is so that if I get an idea while blowing my hair dry, I can quickly scribble it on the mirror. But apparently some people in this house find it "ominous" to step out of the shower only to discover that their wife has scrawled the words "Sweet Valley," "Cut Brake Lines," and "Poison" on the bathroom mirror.

Incidentally, a couple of weeks ago I decided to use Scarlette's bathroom and ended up scrawling some thoughts on the shower wall with her bathtub crayons. Sometimes you're just going along, shampooing your hair, when you feel compelled to write about your innermost demons on the closest surface available to you. Later that night when Scarlette climbed into the bathtub, she looked up at the words and decided to try her hand at practicing her reading, sounding out the words slowly.

"Mommy, what is . . . Suh-AYE-tan?"

That's when I realized Scarlette's bathroom also serves as our guest bathroom, and the fact that SATAN was printed across the wall in bright, primary colors may have possibly been the reason our last babysitter never called me back. These are the sorts of sacrifices my family makes in the name of artistic integrity, in order for me to bring you chapters 2 and 3 of this book.

(Also I may possibly be scarring my children for life. Verdict is still out on that one.)

From the time I learned to read, I lost myself in the worlds I could live in through books. In books, I didn't have to be myself. I could disappear completely into the characters, a reprieve from real life. Then I discovered I could write my own stories. And that was even better. I created adventures for myself, pages of them. In my basement are two oversized bins filled with all the journals I've kept over the years, filled with stories and dreams. My right ring finger boasts a permanent smudge of ink in the indention worn from putting pen to paper. Writing is who I am.

I used to think I was weird. Whenever I watched the classic claymation Christmas special *Rudolph the Red-Nosed Reindeer* as a child, I always identified most with the discarded playthings on the Island of Misfit Toys. I shared this fact with my husband and discovered that he never, in his entire childhood, watched a claymation Christmas special. Then I had to stop everything I was doing to give him an education because, obviously, he could not be allowed to continue living this way. I am such a blessing to that man.

I spent much of my life believing I was a problem. That I was the misfit, the way words always seemed to tumble out of my mouth differently than the way they were arranged in my head, or how I lived out of an overflow of emotion. I've always felt slightly set apart from my own present tense, as if I was both participating and observing simultaneously. The cognitive dissonance between my expectations and my reality left me feeling peculiar in comparison to my peers.

Plus, I had terrible fashion sense. I once wore a hot pink, full-body leotard with Aztec patterned biker shorts and a blazer over the top. I copied the look from a celebrity red-carpet feature in *People* magazine, but as it happens, just because something is considered cutting-edge for movie premieres doesn't mean it gets the same appreciation in middle school math class. I always felt cast away, like the band of broken toys in Rudolph, a social misfit.

Alone on an island.

The silver lining of isolation is that it makes for a lot of time to practice writing. In fact, I wanted to be a better writer, so I gorged myself on books about the art of writing. Somewhere in the stacks of texts that soon began mounting on my nightstand was a thin tome by Anne Lamott titled *Bird by Bird: Some Instructions on Writing and Life*. I had picked it up because I enjoy step-by-step instructions in my life and also because the author wore her hair in artfully arranged dreadlocks. My secret wish is to be able to pull off dreadlocks. I wanted to learn how to write, and what I found in her words was my own reflection staring back at me.

> Throughout my childhood I believed that what I thought about was different from what other kids thought about. It was not necessarily more profound, but there was a struggle going on inside me to find some sort of creative or spiritual or aesthetic way of seeing the world and organizing it in my head. . . . If you are a writer, or want to be a writer, this is how you spend your days— listening, observing, storing things away, making your isolation pay off. You take home all you've taken in, all that you've overheard, and you turn it into gold. (Or at least you try.)[1]

I blew out a breath that felt as though I'd been holding it inside for my whole life. I wasn't weird; I just had my part of speech all wrong. I'd assigned myself an adjective when what I really was, was a noun. *I was a writer.* Honestly, it was kind of a relief, because you can see how spending all day narrating stories inside her own head might make a girl question a few things about herself.

This is my gifting. This is what I was created to do. I simply couldn't see it before, obscured under the veil of self-doubt. I could feel the semblance of it, the way I would sit down to write an essay and get lost in the allure of combining words. From the moment I first learned you could connect the curves of letters together to form a story, I'd been writing them down, filling up marbled notebooks with adjectives and adventures. This is how God works out His purpose in me.

In the winter of 2000, I purchased a teal blue Chevrolet Cavalier with the money I'd earned stocking shelves at the local library. It was two years old, and another year passed before I could drive it because I was terrified of actually getting behind the wheel. But the day I got my driver's license, I drove straight to Jeff's house and offered to take him for a ride.

As we started off, I clearly remember turning and saying to him, "Isn't it great that you don't have to drive me everywhere anymore?" He looked a little pale and replied, "Actually, I was about to ask if you'd let me drive. You just drove on the wrong side of the road through my neighborhood." (Again, if I were British, this would have been totally acceptable.) Ironically, back then he had no idea he would be subjected to my driving for the rest of his life.

I named my car Jezebel, mostly because I was in the middle of reading Liz Curtis Higgs's Bad Girls of the Bible series. Then it broke down in the middle of the road, and I rechristened it Esther because I figured naming my car after a woman associated with wickedness might not bode well for keeping my repair bills to a minimum. I decided to err on the side of the *good* girls of the Bible. And Esther was my favorite of those because of her outrageous courage.

As her story goes, Esther was a small-town girl who happened to catch the eye of the king. So, sort of like the Kate Middleton of the olden days. Except that while Esther did become queen, she still had to live in a harem and was only allowed to see the king whenever he sent for her, because approaching him on her own initiative meant she would get the death penalty. And, as if this wasn't threatening enough, the king also issued an edict to kill all of the Jewish people in his kingdom. He didn't know Esther was Jewish, but still, that royal family was super harsh.

Esther's cousin Mordecai attempted to convince her to approach the king anyway and plead with him to save her people. She was understandably hesitant. She knew the perilous penalties of breaking protocol. This is when Mordecai famously said to her, "Who knows, perhaps you have come to your royal position for such a time as this" (Esth. 4:14). Or, as paraphrased on the hand-lettered print I found on Pinterest, "Perhaps this is the moment for which you were created."

And actually, I kind of feel that way about *this* moment. I realize it's hardly on the same scale as saving an entire population or anything, but I can tell you with absolute sincerity that I think this might be one of the moments for which I was created. "I feel like my entire life has led up to this message, the writing of this book," I told my best friends as I twirled a strand of spaghetti around my fork. "I mean, otherwise what was middle school even for? Actually, I'm kind of like Beyoncé, making lemonade out of my lemons and all."

We are each made for our right-now moments. God moves us into position to take our messy moments and turn them a message of redemption. Esther in the king's court, Joseph thrown into a pit, you and me in the middle of this thing. Sometimes we think everything is falling apart only to find that really, everything is falling together. Every no in our lives is the opportunity for a good and better yes. Every moment of rejection creates a new space in which to be accepted. Every risk comes with a reward if only we let it. When I surrender my own sense of pride and submit to being vulnerable for the sake of the gospel, I diminish the shame. It's in this way that we are free to step into our God-ordained opportunities.

This is your time.

———⚔

When I stand in the back of the room and survey the women in my Mothers of Preschoolers (MOPS) group, I can see it. I can see the way each individual woman was appointed with unique talents and gifts and personalities. I can see how each of us bears good fruit that collectively nourishes our souls when we gather to share our offerings in community. I can see how good we can be together if we'll bear light for one another.

I bet you can see it, too. I bet you can look at the women in your life that you admire, and you can see their gifting, how they contribute so much value into the space around them.

Friendship is my relief valve from the pressure to be a perfect parent, knowing that in the places where I fall short, the women in my life can fill in the gaps. My friend Bre, for example, is an amazing cook. At MOPS she taught us all how to wield a knife and how to make a caprese salad. She also makes an Oreo cake with chocolate ganache icing that could rival all those fancy bakers I watch on *Cake Wars*. I support her gifts by eating her offerings. Every time she bakes something, I'm all, "I volunteer as tribute!"

My daughter's great dream in life is to compete in some sort of baking show on Food Network. She wants to be a chef, and I can barely cut an onion. But over the years, I've devoted much time and energy to the art of cooking, and I do think I'm getting better at it, even though my skills remain pretty basic. I've even found I especially enjoy the preparation of morning meals, when the house is quiet and my coffee is still hot. I spend a lot of time cooking delicious, wholesome breakfasts from scratch.

Somehow, though, this all goes completely unappreciated by my child. Once when she was about four years old, I woke up to find her leaning over the side of my bed with her face next to mine. "Oh, hey, Mommy," she shout-whispered as I opened my eyes. "I looked in da pantry, and I just don't know what da heck we're going to have for breakfast today, so MAYBE you can get me some food from da window!"

"From the window? What?" I asked groggily.

"YOU know, da window! Like when we go in the car, and you talk, and den people give you some food and coffee through da window? You know, like hash browns and things?"

Oh, the window. The drive-thru window. At Chick-Fil-A. Apparently she thinks a good breakfast consists of window food. I can't win for trying.

This is why I'm letting Bre fill this gap for me and teach Scarlette how to cook. I'm going to be her light bearer, and in turn she's going to sow into my daughter's life in ways I cannot. Actually she's done this already. When I was on bed rest for months, Bre cooked weeks' worth of meals, portioned them into daily containers, and drove them to my house to stock my fridge. (My husband may love her for this even more than I do.) But I love it about her, too, the way she gives of her gifts passionately and freely. I reciprocate this by sharing my talents, which is sending her surprise Starbucks gift cards. We all have our gifts.

I'm so glad that Scarlette will have strong role models to look up to in the areas where I'm not strong—like her Aunt Jana's gentleness, and my friend Natalie's steadiness, and my sister's boldness. When we let the women in our lives lavish us with their gifting, we bless one another and relieve ourselves of the pressure to be all the things. (Which is the reason I'm also going to tap my friend Jess to teach Scarlette how to pluck her eyebrows.)

Galatians 6 says, "Live creatively, friends. . . . Make a careful exploration of who you are and the work you have been given, and then sink yourself into that" (vv. 1, 4 MSG). I lived in stories, and now I live out a story. I used books to hide, and now I write them as a cathartic avenue of healing, both for myself and for every woman out there who just needs to hear someone else say, "Me too." This is what I've sunk myself into.

Part of stepping into the boldness of our new identity is embracing our gifts. As women we tend to downplay our talents because the world suggests to us that we should. It's not arrogant to be confident. It's not prideful to embrace your gifts. This is how we help other people flourish. It's all a beautiful cycle, the way we can savor our passions to sustain our souls and unleash them in community to exhort one another, spurring each other on in love. It's how we can take what scarred us and turn it into something soul-stirring. This, in turn, helps us overcome our insecurities as we serve one another. It's also the reason we were all blessed with Adele's *Rolling in the Deep* album.

"You are the ones chosen by God, chosen for the high calling of priestly work . . . to tell others of the night-and-day difference he made for you—from nothing to something, from rejected to accepted" (1 Pet. 2:9–10 MSG).

Perhaps this is the moment for which you were created.

CHAPTER 14

What Are You Afraid Of?

Sometimes the fear of failure steals the
beauty we were meant to create.
—Angie Smith

As a child I was plagued by irrational fears. Actually I'm still plagued by irrational fears because of a little thing called Catastrophic Anxiety. The difference between me then and me now is that as an adult, I know when my fears are irrational. When you're a kid you can't discern the difference between things that make sense to be afraid of and things that are just fears created in your head. Like how almost every morning I wake up to find one of Scarlette's stuffed animals thrown out of her room and into the hallway because she's afraid it might come to life and eat her. It doesn't matter that I've profusely promised her this won't happen. Because she's seen *Toy Story*, she has her doubts.

Do you know what I was afraid of as a kid? Power lines. To be more specific, I was afraid of live power lines that were felled by a storm. I know. It's basically the most common of childhood fears, am I right?

I spent a lot of time imagining that at some point in my life, someone or something I loved, a cherished pet perhaps, was going to be trapped behind downed power lines, and I was going to have to risk my life to dart across the road and grab him, or her, or it. I pictured myself running through the rain as the live wires whipped back and forth around me in the midst of a raging storm. I worried about this often. I worried about my speed and agility. I worried about my lack of spatial perception, as evidenced by the number of times I've backed my car into the quite stationary mailbox at the end of my driveway. I worried about the fact that timing is not my forte. Also, I have short legs. All this worry was for naught, however, because it's never once happened to me. Actually, I've never even seen a downed power line in my adult life.

Quicksand and being poisoned were a few other things I worried about as a child. Just the other night we were watching *Justified* when a main character took a long drink of whiskey. "I bet the glass is poisoned," I told my husband. Then we watched the character keel over.

"The poison was already in the glass," the lady on TV said.

"How did you know that?" my husband demanded.

"I am very well-read," I told him indignantly. By that I mean I used to read a lot of Nancy Drew books as a child, but let's not bother with semantics.

(Plus, he would have known it if he ever deigned to watch *The Princess Bride* with me. Everyone knows the poison is always in the glass.)

I also worried about accidentally getting addicted to drugs. When I was in first grade, we were all ushered into the gym for an assembly about Halloween, in which our childhood innocence was stripped away by authority figures informing us that bad people used needles to shoot drugs into Tootsie Rolls and other such treats. McGruff the Crime Dog sternly told us to "Just Say No," and also to let our parents inspect our candy for drug paraphernalia before we ate it. This led to my parents dutifully spreading out all of the candy we'd collected in our safe, suburbanite neighborhood and throwing out anything that looked like someone had possibly tampered with it. As an adult I wonder if this was all just an elaborate ruse devised by parents to get first dibs on the good candy, but as a child I lived in fear I was going to eat a Snickers and inadvertently become addicted to heroin.

Once when I was about six years old, two little girls approached me by the gumball machine in the grocery store. One of them tipped a bag of fruit-flavored candy toward me and asked, "Do you want some Skittles?" My eyes grew wide and I took a small step back. It was happening. I was being offered drugs. These kids were trying to get me hooked on dope so I'd grow up and never go to college. I knew something was wrong with kids whose parents supposedly let them have candy AND money for the gumball machine at the grocery store. They probably got those quarters from pushing their "Skittles" on innocent kids like me. I was determined to tell those kids, no, I most certainly did NOT want to "taste the rainbow." I had goals in life. I was going to be a famous fashion designer, and anyone who'd ever seen my amazing designs using the Fashion Plates set I got for Christmas would know that.

I took another trembling step backward, raised my hand, and whispered fiercely, "No! I say, no!" Then I ran back to my mother shouting, "Mom! Those kids just offered me drugs!"

She paused her check writing and looked at me in bewilderment. "Don't worry," I told her proudly, "I remembered to 'just say no.'" She looked over to see two little girls pointing at me and whispering to a woman I could only assume to be their dealer.

"I think they were just offering you Skittles," my mother replied wearily. After this she explained to me how to tell the difference between *safe people* offering you candy (other kids, people in your family, the nurses at the doctor's office) and *not-safe people* offering you candy (strangers, drug dealers, and possibly politicians.) I spent the entire car ride home bummed that my fear led to missing out on some free Skittles.[1]

One of the things I disliked the most about myself is that I was so afraid of everything.

People always tried to help me face my fears by quoting 2 Timothy to me. Like this one time I went on a hiking trip and someone squeezed my hand encouragingly on the trailhead, telling me to remember what the Bible says in 2 Timothy 1:7: "For God has not given us a spirit of fear, but one of power, love, and sound judgment."

I was like, "Yes, except it doesn't actually make me any less afraid of crossing this rope bridge that's dangling precariously above river rapids, right next to this sign that has the word DANGER painted on it in large red letters."

In keeping with the biblical theme, I did actually feel quite full of "love" right then—love of being alive. Which is why I used my "sound judgment" to "power" walk myself right back to my car. I think Jesus is super great, but that doesn't mean you're ever going to coax me across a rope bridge. Not even with Scripture.

And yet I constantly felt daunted by that verse. Because if God didn't give me a spirit of fear and timidity then, well, why was I so dang fearful and timid? I certainly didn't want to be, but I couldn't deny or seem to control the anxiety that would creep up on me, always holding me back. The girl I wanted to be was always just out of reach, right on the other side of the cavernous chasm of fear. Fear of exclusion. Fear of imperfection. Fear of being in the water. Fear of getting my pants caught in the bottom of an escalator and being mangled in the machinery. I'm in my thirties now, and I still jump over the bottom step when getting off an escalator. I'm not saying it's logical, I'm just saying I'm afraid of it.

Often on my drive home to where we live now, I have to drive across a bridge. Over water. This would be fine, if I didn't have a completely neurotic fear about the bridge collapsing and plunging me into the lake. I developed this fear when I was seven years old and read a story about this exact scenario in *Reader's Digest*. My grandmother always let me read her latest edition of this magazine when I would visit her because she thought it would be educational. And it most certainly was. It educated me on how I never wanted to drive over a bridge ever again. The way I deal with this fear is to closely watch the cars in front of me to make sure they don't suddenly disappear. If they don't plunge off into the abyss, then I proceed to drive over the bridge. I like to call this A Very Reasonable Plan. My therapist liked to call it an "unsustainable coping mechanism."

We're all just afraid of something. I'm afraid of being lonely, for instance, in addition to the bridge thing. And all the other things. I still struggle to shake the specter of loneliness that haunts my headspace, striking me with the fear that I am the cause of my isolation. This is why the call to live in community resonates so strongly with me, because when we find our belonging, it lessens our loneliness.

Being lonely is not to be confused with being alone, which is something I rarely experience anymore, now that I have children. Scarlette keeps up a steady stream of conversation from the moment her feet hit the floor until the moment her head hits the pillow. Sometimes it doesn't even end then because she's prone to talking loudly in her sleep. My participation in these conversations is both presumed and utterly unnecessary. If I don't answer her, she just answers herself on my behalf.

The other day was one of those days where I greeted my husband at the door with wild eyes and let him know in no uncertain terms I needed ten minutes alone in the shower before I lost my typical angelic disposition. Moments after hearing this, Scarlette came plodding in the bathroom behind me to let me know she fully understood the gravity of the situation.

"Mommy? Hey! Mommy! I am going to help Daddy do all da laundry, and I'm going to go downstairs without my shoes on, because I just want to be barefoot, and dat is okay. Dat is going to be just fine. You don't have to worry about me because I am not going to be in dis bathroom, I am just going to be helping Daddy. And we are going to take all da clothes down-stairs, and I am going to be a big helper with Daddy, and we are not even going to come in dis bathroom because you need your privacy, and we are NOT going to bother you while you are in da shower. Okay, Mommy?"

"Okay, that sounds great, Scarlette," I said, from inside the shower.

So like I said, I'm rarely alone, but this doesn't mean I don't find myself in pockets of solitude, feeling isolated and insecure. Loneliness breeds my insecurity. This is why I am afraid of it, because it plucks at my feelings of inadequacy.

Like all fears, it only succeeds at diminishing me. Fear is our restraint system, a barrier between us and our desires. Fearing rejection keeps me from connection. Fearing judgment keeps me from being vulnerable. Fearing the bridge literally keeps me from getting home in a timely manner.

I thought embracing 2 Timothy meant I would eventually stop being fearful altogether, but more than twenty years have passed, and I've yet to meet a bridge that didn't fill me with dread, even the one I drive on nearly every single day. I do it anyhow because "courage is not the absence of fear, but rather the judgment that something else is more important than one's fear."[2] (This quote is attributed to Ambrose Redmoon, but in full disclosure I heard it first while watching *The Princess Diaries*. You never know what's going to change your life.)

This is how we have the spirit of power and love, by knowing that in our weakness God lends us strength. In embracing that promise of truth, we continue on through our fear. Oftentimes overcoming doesn't mean we no longer experience fear, it just means we keep going in spite of it. We feel fear and we trust God. We feel fear and we ask God to step into that weakness.

Recently someone emailed me to say, "I don't want my family and friends to read my blog. I have no trouble letting strangers read it, but I haven't even shared that I'm writing it with anyone who really knows me because I'm so afraid of what they'll think, and I don't know why."

I wrote back in all caps, "GIRL, I TOTALLY FEEL YOU" because being overenthusiastic about things is my spiritual gift. And also because I understand why she feels that way. This is such a common feeling. We are hesitant to reveal ourselves because we are afraid that people will revel in our inadequacies rather than rejoice in our successes.

One of my girlfriends said to me, "Another thing I'm insecure about is sharing my talents. I have this feeling that if I share something I think is good, other people are secretly thinking, *Why is she even sharing this? She isn't good at this.* This makes it hard to take constructive criticism of any kind because I immediately feel like it's an attack on whether or not I have any talent to begin with."

See? You're not the only one who feels this way. It's a common thread, the way we fear the searchlight of others' opinions.

As luck would have it, one of the good friends who has come into my life happens to be a girl who used to work as a copy editor. She checks over my writing for typos and to ensure it makes sense to other people. She tells me things like, "I think you might have mentioned The Baby-Sitters Club one too many times." (Wrong. You can never have too much Baby-Sitters Club.)

I sent her an email letting her know some areas where I was struggling with my writing because, not that I don't love every one of you reading this book, but it feels a little vulnerable to put all of my insecurities on paper to share with you. By getting a bit of controlled, concentrated feedback in advance, I can hopefully spare myself the indignity of multiplying my mistakes across tens of thousands of copies. So I asked her in particular to help me finesse some places where I felt like I was perhaps being too negative or too up-front. She wrote me back and said, "At first glance, I thought your email read, 'I don't want you to be too negative or up-front.'" I'm sure she was thinking to herself, *Wow, Kayla is going to be so easy to work with. She's obviously very good at taking constructive criticism.*

The thing is, I could spare myself this exposure and misunderstanding altogether if I'd only stay contained inside my fear, if I would keep my writing completely to myself. If we set the bar low, it won't hurt so badly if we fall from it. But almost every time in the Bible where God talks about our gifts, He calls them good. It is only our insecurity that sneaks in and tells us that what we have to offer isn't enough.

Sometimes we hide our gifts from the people we love the most because we know they've seen our flaws. Our insecurity tells us, "I can't place my gifts in front of them when they've seen my past failures." But isn't it actually more likely that your friends—if they saw you exercising your gifts—would cheer you on in eager exhortation? Think about it. If one of your friends told you how they believed God was equipping them to use their gifts, what would you do? You'd most likely be happy for them that they were able to recognize, use, and flourish in their gifting. You wouldn't be thinking, *Well, you were super selfish that one time we went to the beach together in college, so now you have no place doing anything important.* Our tendency is to assume the negative because our fear clouds the truth that our people are for us. That God is for us.

We wonder, *What do I have to offer?* Our gifts *are* our offering. Insecurity is an insidious liar, distorting the truth in our lives and stealing our opportunity to share our gifts as a blessing to others. It nags at us and we find ourselves wondering, *Who do you think you are?*

Emily Freeman writes, "When you finally show up, you will hear this question whisper dark words into your soul. When you are on the verge of discovery, on the edge of risk, when you're ready to take the next step toward influence—this question will come out of nowhere, asking *Who do you think you are?*"[3]

I bet Esther wondered that too.

Emily continues, "Rather than push the question aside or crumble under the implications, demand that it be a reminder of your belovedness. Let it encourage you in your identity. Who *do* you think you are?"[4]

I think I was fearfully and wonderfully made. I think I was created for such a time as this.

I think you were too.

CHAPTER 15

Metamorphosis

*Practice is the hardest part of learning, and
training is the essence of transformation.*
—Ann Voskamp

When my son was about three weeks old, everything felt incredibly overwhelming. Sleep deprivation is intense, and I was deep in the throes of it. (Actually, this book should probably come with a warning label, given that I am prone to writing whole chapters during 2 a.m. and 5 a.m. nursing sessions.) Taking care of a five-year-old, a three-week-old, and our slightly infirm seventeen-year-old dog on hardly any sleep was wearing me thin.

One particular day I was attempting to nurse the baby when I heard a cry from the bathroom. A new antibiotic had been keeping my daughter running for the potty every few minutes, and when I went to check on her, I found she hadn't quite made it there in time. As I was absorbing the scene, I all of the sudden felt a warm sensation trailing down my legs, the result of a massive diaper blowout by my newborn. But before I could even catch my breath, I heard *another* sound—a pitiful mewling sound—and turned to see our sweet puppy scooting down the hallway, dragging her bottom behind her. There was a trail. It was bad.

I had no idea who to help first. In the end I just scooped up the dog and put her in the empty bathtub, because her tiny little Chihuahua legs meant she couldn't jump out. The dog, I figured, was the most likely to spread a mess to the rest of my house, and so my number-one priority was containment. Then I focused on helping my five-year-old. I sat the baby down on a blanket and figured I'd get to him last because, out of the three of us, he was the only one who wouldn't remember this and therefore the least likely to be traumatized. I stood in the hallway, looked at the utter desecration of my house and thought to myself, *Self, your life is a literal poop storm.*

Then I bombarded my husband at work with text messages describing the scene in great detail because the Bible says how in marriage that "two will become one flesh," and so I did not want to deprive him of the opportunity to grow in oneness with me. I am a thoughtful and considerate wife.

Eventually after we were all bathed and everyone smelled much better and my supply of bleach had been depleted, I sat down and caught my breath. I can't lie, I felt a little bit proud of myself. In the middle of that mess, I had maintained my composure.

I once dated a guy who encouraged me to take time to respond to things rather than just immediately have an emotional reaction. This is a very nice way of me saying that he told me to quit overreacting to everything. I have no idea why that relationship didn't work out. It took me some time to learn to temper my emotional responses.

We can't always choose our circumstances, but we can choose who we will be in them.

Once a week, Scarlette attends chapel at her preschool, and a couple of weeks ago I asked her to tell me what she'd learned that day. She answered succinctly, "GOD." So then I prodded a little more.

"Okay, well, can you tell me a little bit more about God?"

She sighed heavily and replied, "Mommy. If you want to know about God, maybe you should talk to Pastor Chad." Touché, Scarlette. Touché.

I do want to know more about God. I'm captivated by the wild mystery that is faith and eternity. But I don't *hear from God*, at least not in the traditional sense.

I'd read a lot of books in pursuit of deeper spiritual life, and I'd noticed how often people reference hearing from God, whether in an audible voice or as a whisper in their heart. I'd never heard God say something to me plain as day. This frustrated me the most when my daughter was in the hospital, and other people would attempt to offer comfort by telling me God had told them she was going to be okay. I felt affronted. If God were going to give anyone some sort of audible reassurance in that situation, I sure would have liked it to be me. Instead, I was met with a supernatural silence. It was not, as the song goes, an easy one.

Throughout my teenage and college years, I thought something in me was broken, like maybe my faith wasn't strong enough for me to hear from God. I filled journal pages begging for God to talk to me. (And also to give me a husband. I had priorities.) I wondered if my tendency to be cynical was keeping me from a divine message.

If I were one of the disciples, I'd probably be Thomas, if only because the adjective preceding his name was Doubting. He isn't the most esteemed disciple, but the truth is that if I were in his position, I can't say that I would have believed in a resurrection either until I too saw the evidence laid out before me. On my own I am completely cynical, sizing up situations with a David Caruso-esque raised brow. On first glance I view everything as suspect. I am a skeptic. This is not a facet of my personality that I am particularly fond of, although it does make me excellent at solving mysteries. I'm basically a female Sherlock Holmes. This is why no one ever wants to watch *CSI* with me.

But in learning about love languages, I uncovered the connection of my heart to God. It made sense to me that if we are in relationship with the Author of our faith, we would receive love in the way that we were created to offer it. For me, I knew physical touch was my strongest sense tied to love (as does everyone whose hair I happen to stroke as I pass them on the way to the buffet at our MOPS group). And in *The Love Languages of God*, Gary Chapman talks about how the love language of physical touch manifests itself as a spirit of worship.

Worship. It makes sense because sometimes when I feel melancholy, I reach for a hymn and the melody remakes me. I don't hear God speak to me in words exactly, but I feel Him when I lean against the couch and watch my husband strum the guitar. God speaks to me in arias, serenades me with Scripture.

Nearly every time I get behind the wheel of my car, a little voice perks up from the backseat asking me to turn on some music. Most mornings on the way to school, it feels like church in that car, with Scarlette's tiny soprano rising over the seats and filling the air with song.

Recently a woman with whom I've just become acquainted told me that God had given her a vision of me. She said she saw me in a storm, holding on to a lighthouse. I was going through a difficult time, trying to keep my second baby from coming as early as his sister did, and her willingness to share this with me was a real encouragement. I don't feel affronted anymore when people tell me they hear from God in such vivid ways. Because maybe, like with this friend, maybe that's how He does it. Maybe for me it's a pen and a guitar, and for her it's an image and a dream. She offered me her gift.

I don't have all the answers. I've been praying fervently for nearly seven years for God to do something in a specific area of my life, and I would love nothing more than a concrete audible answer. Yet in the waiting, I watch for the way Scripture and events in my life fold in on each other and illuminate the path. I lay down my gifts as an offering. I lift up my worship. I trust the Word. I keep the faith.

Part of overcoming means being intentional about what we're consuming. Sometimes we think we're coping when really we're just escaping. I am amazing at the art of avoidance.

If I am not being mindful, I tend to bury my hurts deeply and seal them off, as though entombing them will heal me. I've grown good at compartmentalizing my emotions. I am an expert at feeling numb. But nothing stays dormant forever, and it's usually under pressure that all of the things I haven't dealt with come rushing to the surface. If we simply bury our hurts, we will spill out burning shame like lava whenever we're pressed, decimating everything in our path. It doesn't have to be this way. When we allow God to redeem our pain, we may be overflowing with goodness or spilling out our sorrow, but either way it will be a pouring out of grace.

I remember my youth pastor using an illustration about grapes, telling us that when you step on a grape, what you get is grape juice. What's inside is always what will come out. When I am judgmental of others, I assume that others are judging me. When I am living in grace, I am graceful.

This means different seasons call for different things. When my friends confide in me about a rough patch in their marriage, I tend to recommend that they not read romance novels or watch romantic chick flicks. It's hard to live in the reality of our afflictions, I know this intimately. It is so easy to fill our voids with the fantasy of things that seem better, losing ourselves to what we wish we had. What's intended as an escape becomes a subtle method of underscoring what we're lacking, providing fuel for our discontent.

Consider with care what you consume. Making a conscious effort not to indulge in unrealistic expectations is a healthy way of working through struggles. This is why I don't watch any of those makeover-type television shows anymore, because it tugs at the part of me that thinks a new nose or fuller lips is what would make me happy.

Sometimes when we break free into a new perspective, we end up swinging from one extreme to another. I'm not saying that if you're struggling with comparison you should swear off Facebook. I'm just saying, if you identify that social media is making your heart restless, then it's a good idea to take a small sabbatical from it as you explore why. Whatever your struggle, give yourself the space to examine the cause, and then set about preparing it for redemption.

When Ephesians 5:11 says not to participate in fruitless works, I don't think it's necessarily condemning my affinity for watching all ten seasons of *Friends* back to back with a carton of Ben & Jerry's ice cream. I think it serves as a gentle reminder not to tarry along our path lest we miss what is good by staying lost in the thicket.

When we imagine ourselves before and after, we think of the end of one thing and the beginning of another. But that's where I think we get discouraged because we assume change means becoming someone completely different. Maybe we're looking at change all wrong.

It seems to me that if we are fearfully and wonderfully made in the beginning, then our renewing isn't meant to keep changing us from one old thing to another totally new thing, over and over again. It's meant to liberate us of our shame, enhancing our gifts and adorning us in grace. Transformation, I think, is the unfolding of grace from the inside out. Becoming a new creation is like how a caterpillar becomes a butterfly. It abides there in order to grow into what it was always meant to be. It lets a Creator work over it in its rest, just as when we were formed in our Genesis, in a deep sleep and becoming. And then it emerges to do immeasurably more than before. It stays the same in its essence while becoming a new and better different.

On the other side of the chrysalis, it can fly.

Butterflies don't burrow back into their cocoons; they emerge and they go and be. I would venture to guess that they doubt first. I bet they crawl out of that split-open chrysalis and feel tentative about trusting the weight of their old bodies to their new feather-light wings. They are probably a little bit like Thomas, wondering if he could trust what he couldn't see. But at some point they step off into the air and they take flight on trust of an invisible wind. They are like us, a new creation, and they believe in what they cannot see to keep them soaring.

The Word is our metamorphosis, coming to life within us, and we emerge stretching damp gossamer wings of grace.

CHAPTER 16

Great Expectations

When you stop expecting people to be perfect,
you can like them for who they are.
—Donald Miller

I sort of went through life really believing that love was like a
fairy tale. Or at the very least, a Taylor Swift song. Did you know that in
at least three different Taylor Swift songs the lyrics involve boys roman-
tically throwing rocks at a girl's window? Do you know how many boys
ever actually threw rocks at my window? (Well, okay, one. But that
was because I told him I thought it would be romantic.) Do you know
what this means, other than the fact that I know way too many details
about Taylor Swift's discography? For one thing it means no one thought
through what happens when you throw rocks at an object made of glass.

For another, I think it symbolizes how deeply the idea of an epic love
story is engrained in us.

Judging by all of the Disney Channel Original Movies that I've seen,
I don't think I'm the only girl who longed for a Big Gesture from a boy
in order to feel fulfilled. And I've seen a lot of Disney Channel Original
Movies, y'all. I am definitely an expert on this topic. In fact, the fastest
way to become my new best friend is to strike up a conversation with me
about your love for *Zenon: Girl of the Twenty-first Century*.

(It is such a shame we ended up not actually dressing like Zenon
when we grew up. It's also a shame we don't all live in outer space, but
that's neither here nor there.)

In fact, I've been married for nearly a decade, and I find when I feel discontent, it's usually because I've become restless with the everyday-ness of love. Sometimes it's because my husband is being thoughtless, and sometimes it's because I'm PMS-ing, but most of the time it's because some unmet expectation of mine has left me feeling rejected.

A few months ago, I complained to a friend about a person who wasn't meeting my expectations. My friend gently told me that maybe *I* was the problem. "I've found that most of the time in the workplace, people not meeting expectations is because the expectations haven't been clearly laid out for them," she said. "Are you just assuming they know your needs?"

I, of course, had no idea what she was talking about. I never expect my husband to anticipate my needs without me ever telling him first and then getting my feelings hurt when he can't read my mind. I am a mature adult who communicates sufficiently all of the time without fail. Unless you ask my husband about that. So the more I really evaluated my frustrations, I realized she was right. I wasn't clearly defining my needs. (I also realized she is a good friend because she wasn't afraid to tell me when I was the problem.) Every disappointment in our lives is the result of an unmet need. And when we identify this unfulfilled desire, we create space for ourselves to fill the void with what will heal us rather than trying to put a temporary bandage on the problem.

So now when I'm feeling hurt or lonely or left out, I ask myself, "What is it exactly that I am needing in this circumstance?" Not that asking this question is what I always want to do. What I want to do sometimes is throw my phone across the room. I do not do this on account of how one time I followed through on that feeling, and turns out this is how you break your phone. Getting a little bit introspective is good for the soul and also for protecting your technology.

It's easy to confuse this question, however, by answering it only with things that *others* can do to meet our needs. It's important not to shift the onus of responsibility to other people because other people are always going to disappoint us. It isn't their fault. We are not meant to be completed by our family or our friends or our children or our spouses. We are meant to be completed in God's work. We are meant to complement one another.

This is when knowing your own personality comes in handy. The other night as we laid in bed, I told my husband I needed to hear some words of affirmations from him about certain areas of my life. I asked him to name some things he liked about me. I used to think he should just know when I needed to hear encouraging words, and I expected him to lavish me with them completely unprompted. Now I understand he isn't always completely in tune with my emotional flux, and so I just tell him what I need. "Tell me some things you like about me," I say.

This doesn't mean I never get my feelings hurt. It's just that now I make a conscious effort to assess my emotions situationally and deal with them in a finite manner. As Lysa TerKeurst says, "I can be hurt, but I don't have to live hurt."[1] I don't have to keep reacting to scenarios drawn up in my mind that didn't come to fruition in the way I had imagined. My imagination gets me in a lot trouble, actually. I have to re-center my thoughts and ask myself if the hurt was generated on my end. Did I have unreasonable expectations for this person? Did they say something that triggered a sensitivity in me? Did they make me feel defensive?

We free ourselves from insecurity when we are bold enough to give name to our heart's desire. Nothing grows from a void. We just need to know what to fill it with.

Scarlette is learning the art of preemptive apologies. She recently came running into our bedroom, saying she needed to talk to us. "What about?" Jeff asked her.

"Well, I'm ABOUT to be sorry, dat's what."

I find myself doing this often, preemptively apologizing for myself. I just assume people are expecting something from me other than whatever it is I'm doing, and so I feel the need to apologize for my shortcomings up-front. I bring muffins to my morning mom's group, and I say, "Sorry, these are store-bought," when really I'm not sorry at all that they're store-bought. I'm actually quite grateful to the good people in the Publix bakery for taking the time to package these so nicely for me and letting me pay money for them.

The only reason I'm apologizing for my muffins, which everyone happily eats, is because I assume there's some expectation for me to make them myself. The truth is that none of my friends care if I make them myself. Actually, given my track record in the kitchen, they're probably all relieved to see me bring in breakfast food that is still in the store packaging.

This scenario (and others like it) is the result of my tendency to hold myself to an unattainable standard of perfection. What happens is that I become so obsessed with doing something perfectly that I end up paralyzed by my own expectations. Eventually I just abandon a project altogether because either it will never meet my standards, or I've spent so much time attempting to make things perfect that I miss the window of opportunity altogether.

And that's the story of why the thank-you cards from my baby shower are still sitting on my desk even though my baby is five months old. I *wrote* the thank-you cards. I *addressed* the thank-you cards. But then I kept forgetting to buy stamps to *mail* the thank-you cards. Then once I was off bed rest and able to buy a book of stamps, I felt embarrassed about how much time had passed since the baby shower my friends had been kind enough to throw me. So then I thought I would print out a bunch of pictures of my new baby to include in the thank-you cards, except my printer died halfway through. At the rate I'm going, Ridley will be able to walk by the time I finish these thank-you cards, and then he can just toddle around town and hand-deliver them.

———⚔

I press my lips to Scarlette's forehead because that's the way I measure the heat. I'm shockingly accurate at predicting what the thermometer will say. This ability must have been brought to life alongside my baby during the months she spent gestating, because I certainly did not consider "Predicts Human Temperature within a Tenth of a Degree" among my skill set before becoming a mother. I'm finding it surprisingly useful, however, if for no other reason than when my husband asks me why I can't just use a thermometer to see if the baby has a fever, it affords me a reason to say, "Because, Jeff, what I do have are a very particular set of skills." It's never not a good time to quote a Liam Neeson movie.

The doctor says it's viral, which makes me cringe because I just wasted a co-pay to be told I can do nothing but let the illness run its course. That it will burn up and then die out as fast as it flamed.

Hearing the word *viral* causes me to think of something I learned from Ann Voskamp. I once met her in a hotel hallway and showed her pictures of my daughter on my phone. (I could have used the time to tell her about my latest book but, no, I whipped out photos of my kid instead. I am super good at networking.) Later she took the stage and talked about Internet fame, and how the word *viral* once meant sickness.

I think about this as I scroll through Pinterest, looking for a brunch recipe for a baby shower I'm hosting. The title calls it the Most Life Changing Cream Cheese Spread EVER, but when I click it, I find it's just cream cheese mixed with jam, which is essentially what happens inadvertently every morning when I fix my bagel. And as far as I know, exactly nothing in my life has been changed by it.

Later I see an article that says "This Celebrity Has the PERFECT Response to This Controversy." When I read what her response was, I think it wasn't so much perfect as just really good comedic timing. Which works out well for that celebrity, being that she's a comedian and all.

My friends tease me about my tendency to make exaggerated facial expressions whenever I tell a story, but even I can tell that what fills my newsfeed as I scroll down is just a bunch of overstatements:

This Video of This Person Dancing Is EVERYTHING

At First I Thought This Was an Ordinary Piece of Toast, But at the End I Was Amazed

Taylor Swift's Cats Are the Most Amazing Thing You'll See Today

Link after link of headlines tell me what is "perfect" and "amazing," and each thing is decidedly not. (Although Instagram pictures of Taylor Swift's cats may actually be the most amazing things you'll see today.)

A few months ago I sent my cousin a text that said, "One day I am going to write a blog post titled 'Actually We're All Just Average.'" I love the Internet, but I think too much time on it is treacherous, because it raises our expectations and sets an unachievable standard.

Sometimes toast is just toast.

I think our culture sometimes causes us to stifle our own gifts because we're afraid they won't live up to the hype. When we're inundated with over-the-top suggestions of perfection, it can make our own offerings seem to pale in comparison, leading us to tuck them away. I don't want to go through life like Miss Havisham, the jilted lover of Dickens's *Great Expectations*, limited by my own failed expectations and living in the ruins of a dream. I want to live like Philippians 1:20: "My eager expectation and hope is that I will not be ashamed about anything."

CHAPTER 17

Rewriting the Girl Code

Friendship . . . is born at the moment when one man says to
another, "What! You too? I thought that no one but myself."
—C. S. Lewis

My daughter is going through a stage in which she wants
to assert her independence and be self-sufficient. She also wants to be
helpful, which usually starts out with good intentions but tends to have
fairly poor execution on account of the fact that she's still a preschooler.
Recently she told me, very importantly, "Mommy. I know you think I am
just a little girl, but I am a big girl now, and I can do big girl things!" Which
would have been an excellent argument had she not been attempting to
convince me to let her hold a butcher knife. (She just really loves the
show *Chopped*.)

But she didn't stop there. She kept expressing her frustration that she
felt as though her dad and I didn't let her make her own choices. One of
the things she wanted to do was fix her own drinks. So, okay. We made
her a little basket full of cups that fit in tiny little kid hands, installed a
kid-friendly pitcher in the refrigerator, and showed her how to fill her
own glass of water. Then the following day we put a stack of towels next
to the refrigerator because the only thing missing from this equation was
her sense of dexterity. The novelty has yet to wear off, and every day a

steady stream of water runs between our kitchen and her bedroom. It's like Hansel and Gretel in our house; whenever I can't find her, I just follow the trail of water. I feel like this shows a great dedication on our part at encouraging her quest for independence.

And so it is for this reason that I have no idea why she decided it would be a good idea to fix herself a fresh glass of water from the bathtub.

She walked casually into my office, sipping from the pink plastic cup I use to wash her hair, and I remarked, "Oh, Scarlette, let's not drink from that cup." Because, you know, it just sits on the side of the bathtub, and I figured that while it wasn't dirty per se, it probably also wasn't the cleanest thing ever. (For the record, I haven't always been a germophobe, but six months in the NICU will do that to a girl.)

Scarlette looked down at her cup, walked over to me, held it right underneath my nose, and asked casually, "Oh. You mean because of dis?"

And that is when a huge water bug with about a million legs crawled out onto my face. I cannot emphasize enough how many legs it had or how they were touching my face parts. So, because I am very calm and rational, I screamed loudly and frantically knocked the whole cup/bug combination out of my daughter's hands. Then I proceeded to use that cup to smash the giant bug repeatedly while Scarlette stood in the corner crying, "Mommy, don't hurt my fwiend!" And then I was all, "Scarlette, this is not a friend! This is a foe!" and forced her to brush her teeth repeatedly while I tried to control my gag reflex. It was probably my best parenting moment.

I understood her confusion because sometimes it can be hard to tell the difference between friend and foe. I often see news stories, for instance, pitting two celebrity women against one another as "frenemies." This perpetuates the idea that we can't fully invest in one another, that we must keep people at arm's length in order to shield our own self-interest. But the gospel is never about advancing our own agenda. The gospel is about unity amid diversity, about mercy triumphing over judgment, about natural-born enemies becoming lifelong friends.

True friendship values the people in our lives as community rather than commodity.

———————➤

I forced my friends to talk about this the other day, about friends and foes, about the thirst for community and how it rankles our own struggles with distrust and insecurity. That's the tricky thing about being friends with me. You think you're just going out to a nice dinner, and then, *Bam!*—I'm introducing the hard topics over appetizers because I've got a book to write.

"My secret fear is that no one actually likes me but just sort of tolerates me," one of my girlfriends said, and everyone nodded in agreement. It was a collective "me too," and I was one of the ones nodding the most vigorously. I am always suspicious of this, as though everyone is just secretly placating me by letting me tag along. Interestingly, I myself do not have a single friend that I secretly simply tolerate. I don't even have time to construct that sort of false relationship. Every person I count as a friend is someone I genuinely want to invest time with. That's probably true for you, too. And yet how often do we ascribe a narrative to ourselves that we would never believe of someone else?

"I find I'm a little insecure when it comes to making new friends," my friend Amy told us. "I'm extremely extroverted, but sometimes I walk away from conversations rethinking what I said. Did I sound dumb? Did I share too much? Did I make them uncomfortable? Did I inadvertently offend them? Do they think I'm an emotional mess and want to run away?"

"I'm just not even sure how to make new friends as an adult," my friend Tamika remarked. I get that one too. Seriously, it's not like as an adults we can just pop through someone's fence with our pet bulldog and introduce ourselves. Kids have it so easy.

New neighbors recently moved into the house directly behind us. I discovered this because I was outside playing with Scarlette when I heard a knocking sound, and then one of the boards in our fence flipped up. A tiny little head popped out and called hello to us, as she squirmed through the opening while tugging a bulldog behind her by the collar.

I sort of stared for a minute and then thought, *My life just legitimately turned into a scene from* The Sandlot. Scarlette, however, ran over and introduced herself to the freckle-faced girl, and they have been fast friends ever since.

I don't know if they have a single thing in common, other than the proximity of our houses and a childhood love of sunshine and sidewalk chalk. That sweet girl took the initiative to make an introduction. She was also kind of breaking and entering, so it's possible she's a tiny little delinquent. But it reaffirmed to me something I've been slowly figuring out over the years. The secret to forming friendships is initiation. I don't mean initiation like a sorority style ceremony complete with tea light candles and lavalieres. (Although I wouldn't turn down an invitation to one. I really love tea light candles.)

Friendship happens when someone risks starting the conversation.

Community is such a huge buzzword these days. I can't read a book or a blog post without seeing some kind of emphasis on "cultivating community" or "doing life together." I think it's probably because I was raised in the *Friends* generation, and so we all just assumed we would grow up, move into adjacent apartments, and spend all of our subsequent Thanksgivings getting into hilarious yet sentimental hijinks with one another. Preferably involving Brad Pitt. I won't lie, it was somewhat of a letdown to learn adult life was not so much like that.

Don't get me wrong, I did take away a lot of important life lessons from *Friends.* Just this morning my husband and father attempted to maneuver a couch up our stairwell while I stood helpfully at the top saying, "Pivot. Pivot. PIVOT!" I also know not to count by Mississippis when getting a spray tan. But turns out, I spend way less time sitting on a plush couch in a coffee shop discussing my life than I thought I would. (Weirdly this is not, however, proportionate to the amount of coffee I consume.)

I met one of my best friends when we both signed on to leadership positions for our local MOPS group. The only reason I even volunteered for a leadership position was because I was a lonely stay-at-home mom and I wanted to make friends. I figured volunteering for something would force people to be friends with me, which is pretty much the best reason to volunteer for stuff. Also things about personal fulfillment and community service and whatnot.

We all went on a weekend planning retreat to get to know one another. I went in cautiously and left with a group of girlfriends who would become my core community. I think if I had not taken the risk on that weekend, I might still be lonely. Yet at the same time that everybody's talking about community, I hear women lamenting their loneliness and the lack of a good group of girlfriends. We're constantly connected but we're not connecting. It makes me wonder if community has fallen through the generation gap.

Because at one point in time, people didn't even have to work at it.

My great-grandparents lived in a little yellow house in the smallest of small towns, the type that country songs are written about. It had one stoplight, a Piggly Wiggly grocery, and seven churches all clustered together around the corner from Main Street. Time always seemed to slow down the closer we got to town, and as a kid I half expected everything to turn to black and white once we hit the city limits.

Mamaw Sybil had a shock of white hair that mimicked the cotton fields which sat right across from her front porch swing, where she and her smile were permanent fixtures waving at everyone who passed. I would spend my days working with my great-grandfather in the woodshed, pushing planks of plywood through a power saw, or playing on the skeleton of an old swing set so rusted over that it's amazing I never got tetanus. As dusk fell, my cousins and I would zig through the grass, trapping fireflies in mason jars. And the chairs would be full of local townspeople who stopped by on their evening stroll and stayed for the sweet tea and conversation. "Fellowship," my great-grandmother called it. It was a different time, and not just because apparently no one cared about things like "child safety," as evidenced by both my unsupervised use of power tools and all the times my Papaw Ernest let me drive his Cadillac through town before my feet could fully reach the pedals.

When I think about my great-grandparents' house, I remember the jar of cookies on the yellow Formica countertop, and the way you had to spin a dial on the television set to change the channel, and how we hardly ever gathered around the kitchen table for a meal without a guest at it. That is what I remember the most, the way great-grandparents "did life" with others. Someone was always dropping by with a fresh-baked pie and a prayer. If we wandered down to the lake for a picnic, we always ended up sharing our blanket with our neighbor Miss Nell. When I think about my great-grandmother, I think about how her eyes twinkled, and how she always snuck me a cookie, and the way her door was always open.

Hospitality is the gateway drug to community, and there is this one stage of life that just completely holds us back from it. It's called "My toddler strews bits and pieces of food across the floor like a little Tasmanian devil, and I am way too tired to lug out the vacuum cleaner." This came up over and over again as I spoke to women about our insecurities. On one hand we struggle with feeling left out, uninvited, and unwanted. On the other hand, most of us aren't doing any inviting because we're worried about all the piles of laundry lurking in the hallway. I often think about calling a friend for a spontaneous coffee date, only to then look around my house and decide it would take too long to wipe all the peanut butter off the available surfaces. But hospitality isn't about housework. I know this firsthand because, as we've already established, my housekeeping skills are what you might call "lacking." No, "The heart of hospitality is about creating space for someone to feel seen and heard and loved."

It's easy to talk about it, and really, really hard sometimes to practice it. This is why the door stays closed for so many of us, literally and figuratively. One friend promises she'll start having people over when they finally have money to remodel. Another says she'd be too nervous that people wouldn't eat the food she made, so she never makes the invitation. But it isn't about perfection, and it isn't about performance. You'll miss the richest moments in life—the sacred moments when we feel God's grace and presence through the actual faces and hands of the people we love—if you're too scared or too ashamed to open the door.[1]

When you walk in our front door, our completely unfinished staircase greets you. Usually when people visit for the first time, they set a foot on the plywood steps and ask, "Oh, are you renovating?" Then I'm like, "Yes. Renovating. That's what we'll call it." We've been "renovating" for about six years now, which mostly means we tore out the carpeting on the stairs with intentions to lay down hardwood treads, and then we had a baby unexpectedly at twenty-five weeks, and so we just ended up paying a lot of medical bills instead. It's like my grandma always said, the path to hell is paved with good intentions. Or in my case, the path to my kitchen.

Hospitality begins with intentionality. There's something in the unpretentious honesty of just being ourselves, something in the front-porch openness of simple living, and something in the compassion of caring deeply for others regardless of status or stigma that leads us to everything we really desire in our friendships.

You don't need a squad; you need community.

You need people who would cut through a roof for you.

On one of those days while he [Jesus] was teaching, Pharisees and teachers of the law were sitting there who had come from every village of Galilee and Judea, and also from Jerusalem. And the Lord's power to heal was in him. Just then some men came, carrying on a stretcher a man who was paralyzed. They tried to bring him in and set him down before him. Since they could not find a way to bring him in because of the crowd, they went up on the roof and lowered him on the stretcher through the roof tiles into the middle of the crowd before Jesus. (Luke 5:17–19)

This is one of my favorite New Testament stories, because hidden alongside the miracle of the healing is an extraordinary story of friendship. These friends believed together for a miracle, and they endeavored to work for it on behalf of the one who could not. This is what friendship looks like, when we're committed to carrying each other when one of us is paralyzed.

It would have been difficult just to carry the man through the crowd at all, but they pushed on through the hard things together. And when they were confronted with an insurmountable obstacle, they climbed up on the roof, cut away the shingles, and lowered their friend down, delivering him straight to the feet of Jesus.

Can you imagine? Can you imagine pushing through the throngs of people? I've been to a Backstreet Boys concert, and so I know what it's like to weave your way through a crushing crowd, much less while carrying the weight of another person across your back. Can you imagine the effort of climbing up on a dusty roof in the heat of the day, cutting away the heavy tiles, and hoisting the dead weight of a man up and over the side before lowering him down to safety?

I want to be the sort of friend who will cut through a roof. I want to be the sort of friend who isn't afraid to get her hands dirty in order to come alongside the people she loves when they need it. Sometimes this heavy lifting looks like fitting a cup of coffee into an already packed schedule. Sometimes it looks like being elbow-deep in a sink full of suds so a new mom can sleep. Sometimes it looks like sitting silent in a hospital room. It doesn't have to be a big gesture to be genuine.

I know this works because I've been the recipient of it.

I met three girls in 1997 who would forever change the course of my life: a redhead, a blonde, and a brunette. It almost sounds like the setup of a good joke, except the setting wasn't a bar, it was high school. We were the lucky ones who found a combination of limitless grace for one another when we were still young. Our friendship is the Jonathan and David sort, how "the soul of Jonathan was knit to the soul of David, and Jonathan loved him as his own soul" (1 Sam. 18:1 ESV). It set the foundation for the rest of the relationships that would enter our lives, how we exhorted and loved and forgave. I cannot imagine my life without their group text in it. When I became untethered, it was these girls who threw me a life preserver and reeled me in. In the darkest of storms, they've always been a beacon, guiding me toward the safety of shore. And when I was at my most desperate, they drove me to the office of a trusted counselor and said, "We want this healing for you." They carried me when I was lame. They cut through the roof.

Over the past year the women in my life have shown up for me. They toasted the achievement of my dreams with cupcakes, they cried with me when I got bad news at a pregnancy ultrasound, they bared their hearts for the message of this book, they fed my family and kept me stocked with dry shampoo while I was on bed rest. And I don't think this came about because I am particularly likable or popular. No, it's because within this group of women, we have made a conscious effort to be present for one another, celebrating in the good times, praying through the hard times, and encouraging one another in the ordinary, everyday in between.

These are the real squad goals.

CHAPTER 18

Judgment Day

> Who was I to judge the heart which broke into that
> moment, spilling kindness and longing? Who was I
> to dismiss her story because I did not know it?
> —Edwina Gateley

The experience of motherhood is one that I am exponentially grateful for. After years of infertility, my introduction to motherhood was brought about by an emergency C-section halfway through my pregnancy and a harrowing six months spent in the neonatal intensive care unit. I spent many a day and night next to a plastic incubator watching as a fading heartbeat on a monitor threatened to strip my motherhood from me before I'd ever even held my baby in my arms.

Five years later, I gathered up my newborn son and found myself the unexpected recipient of the great blessing of two children. Some days my heart cannot contain the joy I feel at how lucky I am, because this path was carved out for me by loss and I do not take it for granted. Maybe I'm being overly sentimental about this, but today Scarlette told me that big girls call their mothers Mom instead of Mommy, so I'm dying a little bit inside. I told her she has to be three inches taller before that's allowed, and so far she believes me. (She also believed me when I told her that her baby brother is a robot. The reason I know is because she brought me a spare power cord to plug him in. So I'm an excellent parental example.)

What I'm saying is, motherhood has been one of the greatest gifts of my life. Which is why it confounds me that I care one whit what total strangers think about my parenting skills.

When Scarlette was about three years old, I was sitting on a bench at the park watching her play. She had easily joined in with the other children who were there before us, immersing herself in their games. I watched as she ran with a whole gaggle of kids through the wooden maze of the play set, shrieking with laughter as one of the moms chased them playfully.

A few minutes later, that same woman sat down beside me on the bench and said, slightly out of breath, "Wow, your daughter just loves to have someone chase her." I hadn't yet been acquainted with the concept of mommy judging, and so I naively thought I was wading into a friendly conversation. Spoiler alert: I was wrong.

"Yes," I said, laughing, "Scarlette is under the impression that every-one in the entire world is involved in a perpetual game of chase with her, so this is all of her dreams come true."

The woman on the bench next to me did not laugh. She did not smile. She replied very seriously, "I'm sure it would be such a bonding experience for you two if you were to run with her on the playground." Then she tilted her head, smiled encouragingly and continued, "She would probably just love it if her Mommy was the one chasing her."

"Lady, I chase that child from morning to night. This morning I wrangled her down from the top of the dining room table, where I found her licking the icing off all the donuts I bought the night before. I spend all day running after that kid. That's the whole reason I'm at this park to begin with. So that she can run to her little heart's content and I can sit down without interruption."

Except I only said all of that in my head on account of how Colossians 4:6 says your speech should "always be gracious, seasoned with salt, so that you may know how you should answer each person." I mean, I could defi-nitely be salty about it, but I don't think that's exactly what the author of that epistle had in mind. So instead I just smiled mildly and replied, "Oh, she seems to be having a great time on her own."

The woman stood, shook her head, and said superciliously, "Well, *I* am going to keep chasing them then, because it just brings them so much joy."

Then I was like, "Knock yourself out, lady." (Again, in my head because I am full of boldness.)

I chafed all day under her misplaced judgment. Parenting in public opens you up to an entirely new kind of scrutiny. Discipline in our house is doled out with careful restraint, but when I'm in the middle of the grocery store and my kid hurls a bottle of ketchup on the floor, the frustration boils out of me quick and sharp, my face hot and my words clipped. I don't really even care that much about the bottle being displaced from the shelf; I care about the way the woman across the aisle is watching me and probably thinking I need to get my child under control. I quickly scold Scarlette harshly, even though it's incongruent with how I want to correct her, gently and purposefully.

I lamented this phenomenon to a group of friends. "I'm the opposite," my friend Sarah told me, "I'm too lenient in public because I'm afraid people will judge me even though I know I'm creating inconsistency for my kids."

My friend Jenny chimed in, "I feel like the deck is just stacked against me. If we go out to eat, I feel like people are judging all of my decisions: 'Why can't she control her kid in public?' or 'Oh my gosh, she just lets that tablet babysit her kid.' Either way I can't win, and then I feel insecure, which leads to me overanalyzing and trying to justify my actions to anyone who will listen."

See, you make it out of your school years unscathed, and then you're thrust into the Mommy Wars, which no one even warns you about beforehand. Someone should definitely write a chapter about this in all those baby books out there. Nearly everyone at the table had something to say on this topic, because we've all felt the hot stares of judgment when we're trying to wrangle a crying child through the grocery store. "Someone judging my parenting would reduce me to tears for days. Shame would just abound," my friend Carla told us.

Too often judgment feels synonymous with shame.

Even my five-year-old is judging my parenting. Last night she lost screen time for making poor decisions. A few minutes later she walked into our bedroom sniffling and said, "Mommy. If you just had more EXPERIENCE then maybe I would make better choices!"

So I decided on a mantra to use when I start feeling the heat of judgment and shame in public. I think to myself, *These strangers are going to be a part of my parenting story for about thirty seconds, but I'm responsible to my children for eternity*. My friend Kayla says it a little more pointedly: "I just think to myself, *These people can kiss it*. In the most Christian way possible." (And that is why I am friends with Kayla.)

And that is why I'm feeling a little freer about all of this today.

———✦———

Turn left and stand in front of the big tree across from the playground. They will come.

Those were the directions, typed in stark black bullet points on the page. Those were the only directions. I read the words again; they sounded somewhat like a scene out of *Field of Dreams*. I followed them anyhow, and come they did. I stood there beneath the branches of an old, overgrown maple grasping a cardboard box, and it wasn't a minute before they were spilling out of the doors. They gathered in a semicircle around me, and I put a sack lunch in the hands of the littlest boy in the group.

He took a pacifier out of his mouth to say thank you as he took it from me, and then he turned and toddled off. He couldn't have been more than three years old. It was lunch number 13,401 the food pantry had passed out so far that summer, and the number kept growing as the children kept coming. I handed five bags to a teenager with a little girl wrapped around her knees and two to a pre-teen boy who called me "Ma'am."

And I remembered again what it's like to be in need. I haven't forgotten what it takes to come out of the shadows, and the risk of what you might hear when you do.

I read an article online recently in which a single mother confessed to needing to shop food pantries to make ends meet. The comments section went something like this: "Look at those sunglasses she's wearing. Someone has her priorities messed up." It was mostly sanctimonious criticisms, as though being poor means you should squint in the sunlight.

If you ever want to see shame in action, just look at the comments section of the Internet. I'm afraid for what the combination of anonymity and keyboards is doing to our culture. I would venture to guess that the woman in the article was not frittering away her hard-earned money on inexpensive plastic sunglasses instead of food. I would even go so far as to suggest that maybe she already owned a pair of sunglasses before she fell on hard times, a scenario that doesn't fit neatly into a presumptuous line of judgment typed into an online discussion box.

I cringed as I read it because I know our story. I know we lived incredibly frugally for years and built up an emergency fund as twenty-something-things that would have made Dave Ramsey proud. Then we had an emergency. And just like that, it was gone. A hundred fifty-six days in the NICU will break your spirit and your bank account.

For the first five months of Scarlette's life, she didn't eat. She was fed a cocktail of nutrients intravenously, but her body couldn't process food, not even my breast milk—that liquid gold they praise so highly. I felt like a failure of a mother. First I couldn't keep her in the womb and then I couldn't even feed her. When they finally found a solution her body could tolerate, it came in the form of a predigested amino acid based formula. It cost fifty-five dollars per can. Our insurance refused to cover it.

I sold almost everything in a hastily held garage sale. I sold the antique trunk that I loved, every single DVD we owned, and almost my entire collection of shoes. The last time we had guests over, I looked around for one of our stools to use for extra seating, and then I remembered we didn't have it anymore. I had frantically sold it for four dollars in the garage sale.

And still it wasn't enough.

When insurance denied our pediatrician's appeal for prescription formula yet again, she told me about the WIC office. "They'll give you at least four cans. That will help offset the cost a little bit." So off we went, Scarlette and I—a thin, orange line of tubing running from her nose to her stomach, carried across my body in a sling with a pump tucked in the front pocket.

The logo patterned tennis shoes I was wearing were the only pair I'd kept in the great garage sale purge. My mother had bought them for me for Christmas the year prior and I'd kept them for sentimental reasons, because I knew she had saved up to surprise me with them. I was standing there at the grocery store counter wearing them as I handed in my voucher in exchange for the food my daughter's tiny body needed.

"Buys Coach shoes and uses food stamps for formula," the lady behind me whispered loudly to her husband. *Wait, did I really just hear that?* She didn't notice the dark circles, the way my nails were bit down to the quick, or the red-rimmed eyes that told the story of a mother who cried herself to sleep every single night. She didn't notice the way I stood with my arms wrapped around myself, anxiously shifting my weight from one leg to the other and not meeting her eyes. She only noticed my shoes. She made sure I heard shame.

It wasn't the first time someone had made a comment to me about using vouchers for formula. Nor was it the first time the other cheek I was taught to turn had burned bright red. In all the times I'd shopped for groceries in my life, no one had ever commented on the contents of my cart until I was desperate to feed my daughter.

That's why standing in the park years later, I grant them their space as I turn down the street and stop in front of the basketball goal. The boys shuffle their feet, shifting their weight from one leg to the other, and

I make casual conversation as they take the paper bags from my hands without fully meeting my eyes. Because I remember.

The very last thing I want to do is make them feel ashamed.

It's easy to allow the slights and the shame to swell until we harden, bitter and jaded. But harboring resentment only serves to turn me sour. What I'm looking for is mercy, and now mercy is what I want to freely give.

I slept with one person before I married my husband, and he happened to be the ex-boyfriend of one of my closest friends. It makes my chest tighten a bit to say it, the way insecurity had me so hungry for affection that I became her Judas. I betrayed my best friend with a kiss.

I told her about it sitting on a double bed in a whitewashed cabin in the Blue Ridge Mountains. We were nestled in the valley, and I was even lower, not quite at my lowest but barreling my way down. And she erased it with a word. This singular display of grace made me believe in it, a fountain flowing deep and wide.

Once when I taught Sunday school to senior high school girls, I was assigned a segment on purity. Not long after I gave my outline to the coordinator, I was called in for a meeting. They didn't want me to share the whole of my story, they said, because I didn't seem ashamed enough of the part in which I had once been intimately involved with a man outside of marriage. To be clear, they clarified that I could absolutely discuss it, if only I pronounced my regret more. In fact, they encouraged me in sharing it if only I emphasized the depth of my shame surrounding it.

What I felt, from them, was judgment, like their distaste for my actions far outweighed my sanctification. I felt pinned there, as though they could only see me immortalized in one moment and not as a new creation. Did I have regret? Yes. But if I wanted to pronounce anything undeniably, it was the beautiful overwhelm of mercy and redemption.

I wanted to ruminate on restoration and how through Christ we are made new.

So I respectfully declined. Because what I know about God and the faithful depth of His love is that "he will again have compassion on us; he will vanquish our iniquities. You will cast all our sins into the depths of the sea" (Micah 7:19). What I know is,

> In all these things we are more than conquerors through him who loved us. For I am persuaded that neither death nor life, neither angels nor demons, neither the present nor the future, nor any powers, neither height nor depth, nor anything else in all creation, will be able to separate us from the love of God that is in Christ Jesus our Lord. (Rom. 8:37–39 NIV)

Not even the night I shed my clothes.

I don't want to only emphasize my shame because I've shed that too. The honesty of my story is that it once felt like shame and then, through the literal grace of God, it felt like freedom because it was. It didn't begin and end with misplaced intimacy. That was simply the fallout of a bigger issue: my heart had turned on itself.

They missed the real story.

They missed the deep and the wide.

Life is full of nuance. If I were to assign levels of shame to my own actions, the ones that would make my face burn most are not the ones that remember the heat of hands on my body in that hotel room. It's the memory of sitting in a circle at camp and imitating the girl who wasn't there, my mocking egged on by others' laughter, cementing my making as a mean girl. If I were to assign shame, it would be to those moments in which I stole something sacred from someone else for my own gain because I was heartsick for acceptance.

Sometimes it can be harder to forgive ourselves than to extend mercy to others. Sometimes we assume that people are judging us from afar when really we just happen to be in their line of sight as they squint at the signs in the grocery aisle. And sometimes people pour shame out all over us.

But what I know about God and depth is that it's "for this reason I kneel before the Father from whom every family in heaven and on earth is named. I pray that he may grant you, according to the riches of his glory, to be strengthened with power in your inner being through his Spirit, and that Christ may dwell in your hearts through faith. I pray that you, being rooted and firmly established in love, may be able to comprehend with all the saints what is the length and width, height and depth of God's love" (Eph. 3:14–18).

The key to living in grace is not living bitter.

This is where we find the story within The Story. It's where we get to be the author of our moments, working alongside the Grand Author to highlight the epic parts of an ordinary life and arrange it all on a blank page. (Incidentally, this is also the plot of *The NeverEnding Story*.)

When we have a spirit of forgiveness toward the people who sowed hurt into our lives, we move forward on the path toward change. We can see the *perhaps* when we keep a posture of prayerfulness. Like Joseph said to his brothers, "Don't you see, you planned evil against me but God used those same plans for my good, as you see all around you right now—life for many people" (Gen. 50:20 MSG).

Thank God for grace and change.

CHAPTER 19

Harvest

Let us not get tired of doing good, for we will
reap at the proper time if we don't give up.
—Galatians 6:9

The day my daughter was born was the worst day of my
entire life. This, by the way, is a statement that will earn you a lot of
raised eyebrows if you happen to say it out loud in your Mommy & Me
group. I don't particularly recommend leading off with it if you're trying
to make new friends. I could tell a different story, but my daughter is still
pretty tiny and people ask questions, so it slips out because it's my truth.
Well, that and the fact that I am an over-sharer. My memories of the day
Scarlette met the world are not comprised of happy tears or counting little
bitty fingers and toes. My memories are of how they cut her out of me, slit
me hip to hip, and hooked her to machines as they coaxed her to breathe.

In the middle of the trauma, for just a moment, I was drenched in the
beautiful magic that happens when you bring a child into the world. Then
the joy fused with fear, cloaked in dismal statistics that said this baby I'd
just brought forth into the world probably wouldn't be long for it. And
if she did live, she would likely be deeply scarred by the tragic timing of
her birth. I stemmed a constant, suffocating fear by clinging to a thread of
faith in the doctors, in myself, and in a God I no longer really understood
all that well. She was thirty days old before they allowed me to hold her
for the first time, and as she nestled against me, her heartbeat synced perfectly to mine, because we fit together, mother and daughter.

I loved her immediately and intensely, a love that rolled over me in a flood of emotions like ocean waves, tossing me about and then pulling me under as though I was drowning. My love and fear was all tangled up together because she was here and I loved her. She hovered between life and death, and I stayed in a state of perpetual terror. I was swallowed up in my sorrow, my every breath a petition, my body burning up from the inside out with the intensity of my love and lament. Love for me had so often felt like the loss of things. When my family crumbled and I fell between the cracks. When my husband and I were no longer joined by an ampersand. When I left my baby behind in the hospital for 155 nights. I didn't think that I could bear to risk more love. Once she was well and our home was whole again, I felt utterly content to tend what I had.

And then one ordinary day some five years later, despite the infertility and the prevention and the decision, I found myself staring down at a pink plus sign on a thin plastic stick.

We told Scarlette she was going to be a big sister one September morning before her soccer match. "Oh! Is it going to be a brother?" she asked, bouncing on the bed. "Can I name it Tyler? OR GECKO? That could be a great idea!" I didn't know if the new baby would be a sister or brother. I maintained that I wanted to be surprised, but really I was too scared to find out. I was too afraid of getting attached to another love that might be lost. I was too afraid of being pulled under.

The second time around picking baby names was much harder, mostly because my husband was a little more free with his powers of veto. I offered up Felicity and he vetoed it. He also vetoed Molly and Grace. Apparently he was against naming our babies after my American Girl dolls. I cannot even comprehend why. Those are literally all the best names.

"At least we already have a boy name picked," he said. This was news to me. He had told me back when we were dating that he if he ever had a son, he wanted to name him Ridley. He had decided on that after watching *Gladiator*. I petitioned heavily against it in favor of my husband's middle name, which just so happened to be the name of my favorite soap opera character. (If you've read my first book, you'll know I found this fact quite providential.) But my husband is a creature of habit, and ten years passing did not change his fondness for the name Ridley.

Still, I resisted making the name-picking process any easier by finding out the gender, despite having more than a dozen ultrasounds during my pregnancy. It is quite possibly the most willpower I have ever exhibited in my life. Halfway through the pregnancy my abdomen tightened and the doctors wrapped belts around my waist that sent jagged green lines to a computer screen. I laid my head on the pillow at night and prayed to stay pregnant for one more day, and then I prayed it again the night after until all the nights added up to thirty-six entire weeks. Then I threw out all our possible baby names as they wheeled me to the operating room for my C-section because I am slightly neurotic in everyday life and, as it happens, this trait really intensifies when you are in labor.

They cut into me, steel to skin. I thought about that time long ago when I'd wanted to end my life with a blade and how the sharpness was the way new life was emerging from me now. When they lifted him up and announced I had a son, I wept for the beauty of redemption and for all of the prayer turned to praise. And named him Ridley, of course. You're welcome, Jeff.

I was taken aback by the strength of my emotions. I thought love would rush in like the tide, that it engulfed you whole and you struggled in the swell of it, until you came gasping up for air because of what it felt like before, when love was full of the death of things.

———✍———

Jeff and I, having traced our roots back to Ireland, decided to fly across an ocean to step foot in our ancestral homeland. We climbed hand over hand up a rocky cliff from the base of a waterfall because our guide told us we wouldn't want to miss the treasure that lied at the top. We were wary, the both of us, afraid of heights and the risks of climbing and mingling hearts. We climbed on together anyhow, determined to uncover the mystery of a cliff and of ourselves.

I heaved myself over the lip of the waterfall and stopped short at the edge, the rock dropping off sharply in front of me. I stood still in fear until Jeff turned back to me and asked me what was wrong. "Come see the lake," he called.

"What lake?" I asked him.

He looked at me askance and answered, "The lake right in front of us." The water was glass-clear and so smooth that what I thought was a drop-off was actually the towering cliff above us reflecting in the water below. The danger was only in my skewed perception of the landscape.

We walked around the perimeter of the water, with the cliffs above us and the valley below, and we watched the sun as it rose over the green earth. I stepped back to snap a picture of Jeff as the clouds cleared and light refracted off the water, curving around us in bright stripes of color.

And there we were, standing in the middle of a rainbow. We were finding our way back to one another by the still waters. And for the second time in our marriage, we stood inside a promise.

After Ridley was born, the nurse cleaned him off and laid him on my chest. I marveled at the abundance, the weight of him on my body and the goodness of all things working together. I loved him, and it didn't feel tumultuous like the swelling of the sea. It felt like Ireland. It felt like the peacefulness of still waters and the promise of a rainbow, streaked across the sky. I didn't know love could feel like that. I thought what I had known was all there was of it, that I had made the whole of the discovery. But there is always more to uncover—the ends of the earth and the edges of space and the vast expanse of love. Sometimes we are so focused on our circumstances that we forget our capacity for change, forget that we are not static. We're like water. We ebb and flow to fill out our space and spill over the edges when we are full to the brim.

The name Ridley means "cleared land," and that's what this new season feels like, like fresh earth all turned over and tilled, a springtime arrival of new life and the enduring promise of a fruitful harvest. He reminds me of how we are given a fresh start over and over again. The sun sets and the sun rises and how mercies are new every morning. I rest his head on the crook of my arm, and he curls up against the curve of my body. I let him sleep there, in the hollow of me. (Unless you are my pediatrician, in which case I always put my baby to sleep on his back.) I watch the way his chest moves without machines, and I remain in awe at the miracle of life. I indulge myself in him because it feels like perhaps I was created for such a time as this.

———✦———

We are in the reaping now, the days where we gather up the fruit of our labor and lay out a banquet. This is the season of thanksgiving, for the transformation of seed to sustenance and heartache to happiness. We have seen the provision, and so we invite others to the table because we've spent our days on the threshing floor. We have painstakingly separated our wheat from our chaff, and this is what has restored us, doing the blistering work.

What I wanted was an easy answer. I wanted magic. I wanted prayer to work like a wand, passing over my insecurities and transforming them into something better, desirable. But magic is only the illusion of things. Ball gowns and carriages turn back to rags and pumpkins at the stroke of midnight. We are not transformed as if by magic. We are transformed by our faithful laboring, the repetition of sowing life-giving words back into our souls to take root deep within us. We are transformed by the renewing of our minds. We are transformed when we keep showing up, long past the midnight hour, tending our mustard seeds of faith.

We are transformed by creating space in our seasons for God to do the supernatural. And in this way we are restored. What shame has scorched, God redeems as beauty from the ashes.

> The Lord is my shepherd; I shall not want.
> He makes me lie down in green pastures.
> He leads me beside still waters.
> *He restores my soul.*
> (Ps. 23:1–3 esv)

CHAPTER 20

Flourish

Isn't it nice to think that tomorrow is a new
day, fresh with no mistakes in it yet?
—L. M. Montgomery, *Anne of Green Gables*

There is such a beautiful dichotomy between darkness and light, the way one cannot exist without the other. The beauty in the vast expanse of stars is revealed to us only because they shine against the inky black of a night sky. You capture a picture by measuring light, but you can't see it until it's exposed in the darkness. We live in the balance of this polarity. We are always choosing one or the other.

I realize you may have assumed here that I'm setting up a touching, heartfelt story about how God lights a path for us in the darkness. But, no. This is a story about the time Scarlette stole my flashlight. I mean, it's true of God too, but it's also true that I really needed that flashlight.

What you may not know about me is that I live in an area of the South known as Tornado Alley. I am deathly afraid of tornadoes, so don't ask me why I still live here. I don't even know. I ask myself this same question every time I'm huddled under a mattress in the basement as the sirens go off and the newscaster is urging me to take cover. (He's always way too late on that advice. If it looks like it might possibly rain, I'm already setting up camp down there.)

Some people like to call the back room in our basement the "playroom," but really its main purpose is to serve as my Tornado Safety Room. Yes, it houses toys and a few musical instruments that I relegated to the one place in the house where noise doesn't carry (and a heartfelt thank-you to the person who gave my child a drum set), but really its function is to provide me peace of mind in case of a tornado.

When I was eight years old, our house was hit by a tornado, and I still have very vivid nightmares about that day, huddling in the basement with my family as the trees crashed down and trapped us. After that, I developed an intense fear of storms. I grew up a latchkey kid, and occa-sionally my parents would arrive home after work to find me cowering in the corner of the basement when it was merely drizzling outside. Probably they should have gotten me some sort of therapy.

That's why I keep a stash of flashlights, battery-powered radios, water bottles, and protein-infused snacks next to a stack of blankets and spare flip-flops in the basement. In case I ever get trapped in it. This is equal parts neurotic and logical.

I also keep an excessive amount of flashlights stashed around the house, in case I ever need to make my way to my Tornado Safety Room in the dark. This is just good planning. My family likes to mock me for my overabundance of flashlights, to which I like to say, "No one lights a lamp and puts it under a basket, but rather on a lampstand, and it gives light for all who are in the house." That's from Matthew 5:15. My flashlight obsession is totally biblical.

("If by biblical you mean, 'of biblical proportions' then, yes," said my BFF.)

Something you should know about Scarlette is that she enters a room like Kramer from *Seinfeld*. She flings the door open and throws her whole body forward with an incredible amount of enthusiasm. That's how the hole in the wall got there, because at some point she removed the door-stop (I don't know why she removed the doorstop or what she did with it) and then flung herself through the doorway with enough force to cause the doorknob to go right through the drywall.

The reason I mention all this is because when my husband asked Scarlette to return the flashlight he'd seen her sneaking out of my drawer earlier in the day, that's when we learned that Scarlette had turned the flashlight on and then promptly proceeded to drop it down the hole in the wall. (Actually come to think of it, that might be what happened to the doorstop.)

Naturally, I worried it might burn the house down. And I spent a good amount of time fretting about that scenario until my husband assured me we definitely did not need to spray the fire extinguisher into the wall. (I'm still not sure his assessment of that situation was entirely accurate.) Then I thought about that trapped beam of light just stuck down between the studs of the walls until the batteries burned out, and how it seemed like such a waste of a perfectly good flashlight. Sort of like lighting a lamp and putting it under a basket.

And so, every day as I peeked in to see if the light was still shining, the more I began to feel like that little flashlight wedged between the bones of my house was a symbol, a reminder of what the Word promises us.

I love the way *The Message* phrases that verse in Matthew:

"Here's another way to put it: You're here to be light, bringing out the God-colors in the world. God is not a secret to be kept. We're going public with this, as public as a city on a hill. If I make you light-bearers, you don't think I'm going to hide you under a bucket, do you? I'm putting you on a light stand. Now that I've put you there on a hilltop, on a light stand—shine! Keep open house; be generous with your lives. By opening up to others, you'll prompt people to open up with God, this generous Father in heaven." (Matt. 5:14–16 MSG)

The truest way toward reconciliation is to be open to God's illumination. And then our instruction is to shine. In being generous with our lives, we're able to create the community we crave.

Light gives us all something to navigate by.

My friend Lisa asked me if I'm uncomfortable having so many people know so many intimate details about my life. Mostly I'm just nervous about my dad reading that one chapter about sex. The truth is, yes, it is scary to be vulnerable on paper, to expose yourself and then send it out to the world. One of my favorite quotes is by Anne Lamott who wrote, "Toni Morrison said, 'The function of freedom is to free someone else,' and if you are no longer wracked or in bondage to a person or a way of life, tell your story. Risk freeing someone else."[1]

This is my prayer, that by opening up to others I will prompt people to open up with God because I know the hope that light brings. I know that "the light shines in the darkness, and the darkness has not overcome it" (John 1:5 NIV).

But no one tell Scarlette her shenanigans happen to be filling my soul with Scriptures.

I have this dream that one day my house will be filled with plants—ivy and peace lilies and maybe a fiddle-leaf fig in the corner. HGTV has made me very much desire to possess a fiddle-leaf fig. The problem with this is that I cannot seem to keep a single indoor plant alive. My friend Breanna once gave me a succulent in a little hand-painted mug, and two weeks later it was blackened and brittle because I accidentally set it on fire.

"I think I killed my succulent," I texted her.

"I would think so, since you set it on fire," she replied. "I'm pretty sure that kills plants."

Word to the wise: do not sit live plants very close to candles.

About two years ago, I tried again with a miniature flowering cactus plant. I brought it home and sat it on a high shelf in my kitchen. Only the bright pink flower peeked over the brim, the cactus itself obscured from view at that height. I would occasionally tip a little bit of water in, smiling to myself about how I was finally keeping a plant alive. Just the other week when my mother was visiting, I mourned aloud the loss of my African violet plant, which I had faithfully tended only to watch it shrivel up despite all my careful devotion. "Well, at least I've still got the cactus," I told her, "I've kept that thing alive for two entire years. It is literally my only success story."

Last night I was scrolling through some article on the Internet when a picture caught my eye. It was a tiny little cactus plant with a bright pink flower. "Someone glued a fake flower on this live cactus!" the caption read.

Wow, I thought to myself, *that is a really good fake cactus flower. That looks exactly like my flowering cactus, except mine is real.*

Mine is . . . real, right?

A few seconds passed before the sinking realization hit me.

"Nooooooo!" I wailed. I stood and walked to my kitchen, slowly and somberly. I pulled over a stool and then reached up onto the shelf and took down my beloved cactus plant. There inside sat a few pointy spikes and one pink flower that was decidedly not real. My beloved cactus flower was a fake. There wasn't even an actual cactus anymore; it had at some point in time disintegrated into the dirt. I don't even know when that happened. Probably about one year and eleven months ago. All that was left was a fake flower and the now visible clump of hot glue that had once attached it to my plant.

I immediately texted my best friends, "I am having a crisis of faith! I don't even know what is real anymore!" I am very practical and never over-exaggerate.

You know what this means, don't you? It didn't really matter how much I watered that cactus flower or that I kept it sitting in the sunlight. It was never going to flourish because it wasn't real. It was pretty and seemingly perfect, but it had no roots and it had no life. It was the worst sort of deception because I saw in it what I wanted to see instead of what it was. I let it die, untended, because I never took it off the shelf to really look beyond the surface. Also because I can't actually reach that shelf without a stool, but that's beside the point.

I don't want to pass myself off as prosperous when I'm really just barely hanging on like a pink paper cactus blossom. I want to live the way the psalmist wrote, "The righteous flourish like the palm tree and grow like a cedar in Lebanon. They are planted in the house of the LORD; they flourish in the courts of our God" (Ps. 92:12–13 ESV).

I want to be shameless, and I want to flourish.

———

I was blaring the Dixie Chicks as I swept the floors, but unlike the song I was singing, it was not a cold day in July. It was a blazing hot day in July because I live in the South, where the expression for a summer day is, "It's hotter than hell and half of Georgia." The thing about that is, I live in half of Georgia. It's real hot, y'all.

I heard the door open, but didn't hear it close, and then I had a sort of out-of-body experience as I watched myself physically turn into my mother and yell, "Shut the door RAT NAO! You're letting all the cold air out!" Scarlette came trudging in, sweaty from tennis camp and dragging her faded orange school bag full of tennis gear behind her.

That orange school bag. For several weeks in the spring, Scarlette had complained she couldn't carry it because it was too heavy. What she specifically said to me was, "It's SO heavy and I don't know why! I'm too little for this! I don't want this to happen to me!" As you might have noticed, Scarlette is super low-key all the time, just real chill and never melodramatic.

To the best of my knowledge, her school bag usually contained a single folder and a water bottle, which she'd toted around for two years without a single problem, and so when started complaining about how heavy it was, I summarily dismissed her complaint and instructed her to drape her bag over her shoulder as per usual. What followed was that she would dramatically heave it down the stairs, with lots of exaggerated sighing and loud grumbling about said heavy bag after I'd made her carry it anyway. Mama don't play. But when all the grousing failed to cease, I decided to investigate the matter, whereupon I opened her school bag to discover that Scarlette had filled it with rocks.

Rocks!

This left me speechless. Because there were so many other solutions to her problem. She could have emptied the bag. She could have explained to me why the bag was heavy, and I would have removed all the rocks for her. Instead, she chose to trudge up and down the stairs lugging a bag full of unnecessary heaviness around, because at some point she decided to hold on to something that she never really needed in the first place.

(Additionally, I could be an engaged parent who checks her child's school bag more than once a week but that's neither here nor there.)

Shame is like a stockpile of stones that weigh us down. It dries us up until we're nothing left but thorns atop the soil. It forbids us from flourishing.

But we don't have to bow under the weight of our accumulated hurts. We don't have to live heavy-hearted. You might know what is coming next, but don't skip over it out of familiarity because every measure of this verse is a treasure:

> "Come to me, all of you who are weary and burdened, and I will give you rest. Take up my yoke and learn from me, because I am lowly and humble in heart, and you will find rest for yourselves. For my yoke is easy and my burden is light." (Matt. 11:28–30)

It's the middle portion of this verse that I am most taken with, the part where we are called to learn. "Learn from me," Jesus says, because He knows the secret to being unburdened is to believe in truth. He doesn't say "hear me." He says "learn from me," prompting us to take His promises and apply them to how we live. *We learn*. And under this divine tutelage, we become a new creation. *We flourish*.

In our new creation we can live the way the psalmist sang, "He is like a tree planted by streams of water, that yields its fruit in its season, and its leaf does not wither" (Ps. 1:3 ESV). This is the way the psalms begin, in the first chapter, reminding us how to flourish.

I don't have any fruit trees because apparently our homeowner's association is against things like delicious fruit and line drying your cloth diapers. Which is why I put my clothesline and blueberry bushes in the backyard and then bribed my neighbors into silence with baskets of fresh blueberry muffins. Allegedly. I do have a set of blueberry bushes though, because they produce best in pairs, and a line of strawberry plants marching down a mound of earth that sits below our bedroom window. For all the care I give them they only bloom in the spring. We cover over them in the winter so that they can come back again, stronger and yielding fruit in their season.

Our life cycle is created for rhythms of fruitfulness and rhythms of rest. We have seasons of change and seasons of growth and seasons of harvest. "For everything there is a season, and a time for every matter under heaven" (Eccles. 3:1 ESV) The earth spins slow on its axis, the rotation turning night into day and the sun rises and the sun sets. We fall asleep and we wake up to a new morning bright with the possibility of change and the promise of new mercies. This is the wild mystery of faith that steadies in an ever-changing world. Life is not stagnant, the essence of it carries us ever forward and we are always in the process of becoming. I thought this was the weakness; that I was never complete meant that I was never satisfactory. But as my friend Ruth says, "You don't have to be blooming to be growing so don't give up."[2]

I'm still me. I am the sum of all of my experiences, the times I have loved and the times I have lost. My sense of humor is still mostly facetious, and I still struggle to find my car keys. But I am abiding. I no longer live in shame. The old things have passed. I am consecrated to a calling. The new things have come. I am the same, but a new and better different.

She is a new creation.

The old has passed away; behold, the new has come.

Acknowledgments

You'll likely find it shocking to learn that when faced with an important task I have a tendency to procrastinate terribly.

That is maybe what happened with this acknowledgment section.

I kept putting off writing it, if simply because the breadth of my gratitude for every piece of this project is so immense that it almost felt paralyzing. If I felt lucky to write one book, then writing two was beyond anything I'd dared to hope for. Encapsulating my appreciation in a few paragraphs seemed an insurmountable task.

(Plus, I already thanked Ann M. Martin unironically in my first book and so I sort of felt like I peaked after that.)

This particular book was bound together by the generosity of so many people who gave of themselves—of their time, and their talents, and their teary-eyed confessions. It was stitched together through shared stories, spilled out secrets, and a hollowed out space waiting to be filled with a hallowed measure of grace.

Writing this book was a gift and I am grateful.

So this is to you. For walking alongside me through this story, one that asked you to confront the things we find most haunting and stare into the shadows of feelings long left buried. I'm so grateful to you for entrusting me to stir it all up as you turned the pages forward. (Plus, that was a lot of adolescent angst you just read. I really feel like you should be commended for that.)

It's to every woman who graciously gave me their stories to grace these pages in hopes that they would mend the hearts of strangers.

To my MOPS group, who taught me what it means to show up, to press in, and what it looks like to always have a seat at the table.

To my CAG friends, who are the very definition of competition and yet choose to be cheerleaders in our calling to this craft.

To Crystal, Jennifer, Wendy, Erin, Jen, Kelly, and Teri Lynne, who lent their voices to champion this message and in turn encouraged my heart.

To Kristen and Lisa, who read all the rough drafts and still stayed friends with me.

To the team at B&H, who I feel incredibly blessed to partner with because of the way they communicate grace across people and pages and their commitment to so much more than books.

To Lawrence, who I owe more than I can say for taking what I thought was broken and restoring it in such a way that helped me see grace spark to life on the pages.

To Jenni, who has never left my corner even when I doubted I belonged in it.

To Tiffani, Natalie, Laura Anne, and Breanna, who at various times in my life carried me but never called it a burden while they cut through a roof.

To my family, who maybe are a little mortified that I chose a career where I tell so many embarrassing stories about us but are still so supportive and also probably keeping my books in stock solely through their sheer pride.

To my sister, who kept me fueled for long nights of writing while tending to a newborn with hilarious text messages and also for not telling our parents about that one time I tried to lose you in the forest.

And to Jeff, for long drives with the T-tops off to two babies and all of the in between.

Study Guide for Individuals and Small Groups

Transformation in my life came about through a combination of heart work and physical work. We are going to come together to find our renewal at the intersection of these things. You will need a journal to complete the work below, which you'll see is divided up into four-chapter sections. Visit inbloombook.com/extras to download journaling pages, Scripture affirmations, and other fun extras!

Chapters 1–4

Affirmation

What you say about yourself means nothing in God's work. It's what God says about you that makes the difference. (2 Cor. 10:18 MSG)

Conversation

* Share the statement(s) in these four chapters that resonated the most with you. Why did they speak to you?
* What is the origin point for your shame or insecurity? How has that shaped the way you live and interact with others?
* How does self-worth manifest in your life? Would you describe it as positive or negative?
* How do you feel about yourself? Do you speak love to yourself or does criticism dominate your inner voice?

Transformation

* Print out the scriptural affirmations found at the link above. Memorize and meditate on them. Hang them up where you need them most!
* Start a journal and keep a record of the areas in your life that are triggering feelings of shame or inadequacy within you. At the end of the week, evaluate each instance to see what situations or thoughts are causing them. What are some ways that you can change these for the better?
* Go through each instance in your journal and pair it with a scriptural affirmation that speaks to it. Each time you are confronted with a negative thought, stop and meditate on the truth.

Chapters 5–8

Affirmation

You'll be a stunning crown in the palm of God's hand, a jeweled gold cup held high in the hand of your God. No more will anyone call you Rejected, and your country will no more be called Ruined. (Isa. 62:3–4 MSG)

Conversation

* Share the statement(s) in these four chapters that resonated the most with you. Why did they speak to you?
* In what areas do you struggle with self-esteem or self-doubt?
* How do you deal with rejection?
* Do you fear abandonment? How does this manifest in your life? How does this impact your relationships?

Transformation

* Print out the journal pages and the Scripture affirmations found at inbloombook.com/extras. Pair each "I feel" statement with an affirmation of truth to meditate on. (Example: "I feel

unattractive." God says, "You shall be a crown of beauty in the hand of the LORD." —Isa. 62:3 ESV)

* If you struggle with shame from past relationships, read 2 Corinthians 5:17–19 and commit to reading it aloud daily.
* Reflect on how you handle instances of rejection. How do they make you feel? How do you react to those feelings?
* Memorize and meditate on Deuteronomy 31:6 and Hebrews 13:5.

Chapters 9–12

Affirmation

For we are God's handiwork, created in Christ Jesus to do good works, which God prepared in advance for us to do. (Eph. 2:10 NIV)

Conversation

* Share the statement(s) in these four chapters that resonated the most with you. Why did they speak to you?
* How does envy erode your relationships?
* What areas do you seek validation in? How does that affect your relationships? How does it affect how you see yourself?
* What comparisons do you find yourself making? In what areas do you struggle with feeling like you don't measure up?
* What is your love language? What does love feel like to you?

Transformation

* Visit 16personalities.com and take the personality quiz.
* In your journal, list the ways you give and receive love.
* Identify a relationship that envy encroaches on in your life. Write down three fruitful steps you can take to replace envy with empathy, kindness, or love.
* Read Proverbs 31. In what ways did you relate to this passage of Scripture in the past? Discuss new takeaways after reading this passage framed as a blessing.

Chapters 13–16

Affirmation

Therefore, if anyone is in Christ, he is a new creation; the old has passed away, and see, the new has come. (2 Cor. 5:17)

Conversation

* Share the statement(s) in these four chapters that resonated the most with you. Why did they speak to you?
* What do you think your gifts are? How are you using them? How do you think others see your gifts?
* In what areas of your life would you most want to experience a transformation?
* Do you believe you are a new creation? If not, what keeps you from embracing grace in your life?

Transformation

* In your journal, keep a record of the time you spend on social media for one week. Then, take a week-long social media sabbatical. Write down how you spent the time differently and how it made you feel.
* In your journal, list each area of gifting that you see in your life. What are you passionate about? What are your talents? If you are studying this in a group setting, have others speak to what kind of attributes they see in you. Write down ways that your gifts can be used fruitfully.
* My friend Stacey Thacker suggests keeping a list of examples of God's faithfulness to you in the past. Start a fresh page in your journal to write down where you have seen God work in your life. How do you see these themes in your present?
* Set a goal to initiate time with a friend this week.

Chapters 17–20

Affirmation

She is clothed with strength and dignity, and she laughs without fear of the future. (Prov. 31:25 NLT)

Conversation

* Share the statement(s) in these four chapters that resonated the most with you. Why did they speak to you?
* How do you feel about friendship? How do you feel about the relationships in your life?
* What area in your life do you feel judged in?
* What things in your life are preventing you from flourishing?

Transformation

* Write down the areas that you feel judged in. Match an affirmation to each instance and meditate on it.
* Ask a trusted friend to help you work through the area of shame in your life by listening to your story and helping to point out the areas of blamelessness in you.
* Read back through your journal. What lies have you been able to replace with truth?
* Share your flourishing by sending encouragement to someone else this week!

Notes

Introduction

1. Brené Brown, *The Gifts of Imperfection* (Center City, MN: Hazelton, 2010), 39.
2. Elisa Pulliam, *Meet the New You* (Colorado Springs, CO: Waterbrook, 2015), 1, 5.

Chapter 1

1. Marianne Williamson, *A Return to Love: Reflection on the Principles of "A Course in Miracles"* (New York: HarperCollins, 1992).
2. Spoken by Tom Hanks in *Forrest Gump* (Paramount Pictures, 1994).

Chapter 2

1. Lysa TerKeurst, *Uninvited: Living Loved When You Feel Less Than, Left Out, and Lonely* (Nashville, TN: Nelson Books, 2016), 8.

Chapter 3

1. Matthew 4:1–11; Mark 1:12–13; Luke 4:1–13.
2. Interview with Curt Thompson by Rob Moll, "How Neuroscience—and the Bible—Explain Shame," *Christianity Today* (June 23, 2016).
3. List of affirmations used with gratitude from *Christianity Today*; http://www.christianitytoday.com/iyf/faithandlife/devotionals/what-does-bible-say-about-me.html.

Chapter 5

1. I wrote a similar account of this story on my blog at *Kayla Aimee Writes*, "Do You Think You Can Handle That?" (August 6, 2015); http://kaylaaimee.com/do-you-think-you-can-handle-that.

Chapter 6

1. Heather Davis Nelson, "10 Things You Should Know about Shame," *Crossway* (June 20, 2016); https://www.crossway.org/articles/10-things-you-should-know-about-shame/.

Chapter 7

1. Kaitlyn Bouchillon, "For the Girls with Thighs That Touch," *It Just Takes One*, July 2014; http://kaitlynbouchillon.com/2014/06/for-the-girls-with-thighs-that-touch/.

Chapter 8

1. Curt Thompson, "How Neuroscience—and the Bible—Explain Shame," *Christianity Today* (June 23, 2016); http://www.christianityto-day.com/ct/2016/julaug/how-neuroscience-and-bible-explain-shame.html?start=2.

2. See another version of this story at Kayla Aimee, "When Your Marriage Is a Shade of Grey," *The Better Mom* (August 10, 2015); https://www.thebettermom.com/blog/2015/8/10/when-your-marriage-is-a-shade-of-grey.

3. Kayla Aimee, *Anchored: Finding Hope in the Unexpected* (Nashville, TN: B&H Publishing, 2015), 118.

4. I wrote a version of this story on my blog at *Kayla Aimee Writes*, "The Echoes of Prematurity" (June 22, 2015); http://kaylaaimee.com/the-echoes-of-prematurity.

5. I adapted my vows from Donald Miller's *Blue Like Jazz* (Nashville, TN: Thomas Nelson, 2003).

Chapter 11

1. Erin Loechner, "Well Done," *Design for Mankind* (August 19, 2016); http://designformankind.com/2016/08/comparison-among-moms/.

2. Amy Poehler, *Yes, Please* (New York: HarperCollins, 2014), 32.

Chapter 12

1. Thanks to Rachel Held Evans for first introducing this concept to me in her article "3 Things You Might Not Know about Proverbs 31" at https://rachelheldevans.com/blog/3-things-you-might-not-know-about-proverbs-31.

2. Amy Poehler, "In One Perfect Sentence, Amy Poehler Schools a Guy in What It's Like to Be a Woman," Mic.com (August 27, 2014),

https://mic.com/articles/97464/in-one-perfect-sentence-amy-poehler-schools-a-guy-in-what-it-s-like-to-be-a-woman#.j3Anpdiwm.

3. Kathleen Norris, *The Cloister Walk* (New York: The Berkeley Publishing Group, 1997), 60.

4. Shauna Niequist, *Cold Tangerines: Celebrating the Extraordinary Nature of Everyday Life* (Grand Rapids, MI: Zondervan, 2007), 15.

Chapter 13

1. Anne Lamott, *Bird by Bird: Some Instructions on Writing and Life* (New York: Anchor Books 1995), 66.

Chapter 14

1. A version of this story first appeared on my blog at *Kayla Aimee Writes*, "Taste the Rainbow: Halloween Candy and That Time I Was Offered Drugs" (October 29, 2012); http://kaylaaimee.com/halloween-candy-and-drugs.

2. Courage quote taken from Ambrose Redmoon's article "No Peaceful Warriors!" *Gnosis* (1991).

3. Emily P. Freeman, *A Million Little Ways: Uncover the Art You Were Made to Live* (Grand Rapids, MI: Revell, 2013), 142–43.

4. Ibid.

Chapter 16

1. Text originally tweeted by Lysa TerKeurst in 2016.

Chapter 17

1. Shauna Niequist, *Bread and Wine: A Love Letter to Life Around the Table with Recipes* (Grand Rapids, MI: Zondervan, 2013), 109.

Chapter 20

1. Anne Lamott, *Bird by Bird: Some Instructions on Writing and Life* (New York: Anchor Books, 1995), 193.

2. Ruth Chou Simons, *Gracelaced* (Eugene, OR: Harvest House, 2017), 58.